Alternative
Computers

Other Publications:
AMERICAN COUNTRY
VOYAGE THROUGH THE UNIVERSE
THE THIRD REICH
THE TIME-LIFE GARDENER'S GUIDE
MYSTERIES OF THE UNKNOWN
TIME FRAME
FIX IT YOURSELF
FITNESS, HEALTH & NUTRITION
SUCCESSFUL PARENTING
HEALTHY HOME COOKING
LIBRARY OF NATIONS
THE ENCHANTED WORLD
THE KODAK LIBRARY OF CREATIVE PHOTOGRAPHY
GREAT MEALS IN MINUTES
THE CIVIL WAR
PLANET EARTH
COLLECTOR'S LIBRARY OF THE CIVIL WAR
THE EPIC OF FLIGHT
THE GOOD COOK
WORLD WAR II
HOME REPAIR AND IMPROVEMENT
THE OLD WEST

This volume is one of a series that examines
various aspects of computer technology
and the role computers play in modern life.

Alternative Computers

BY THE EDITORS OF TIME-LIFE BOOKS
TIME-LIFE BOOKS, ALEXANDRIA, VIRGINIA

Contents

1

2

3

The Analog Option

In 1945, while serving as a consultant to the designers of a pathbreaking computer called EDVAC, the eminent mathematician John von Neumann wrote a memorandum that would be seen almost as a manifesto of a new age. The memo was essentially a description of the machine. Among other features, he said, EDVAC would be electronic, would work with binary numbers, and would act on program instructions sequentially, or one at a time, by means of a kind of logic engine (later called a central processing unit, or CPU). So great was the mathematician's stature in the scientific world that, although his role on the project was merely advisory, the list of characteristics became known as von Neumann architecture. It was, in any event, epochal. Over the next three decades, computers much faster and more powerful than EDVAC were developed, but with few exceptions they worked in precisely the same way.

But in time, one feature of such machines grew worrisome. Sequential operation gained the label "von Neumann bottleneck"; vast numbers of instructions were forced to march single file through the CPU, limiting computing speed.

Advances in electronics alleviated the problem by permitting the central processing unit to deal with each instruction in ever-shorter slices of time. But the bottleneck was inherent in the von Neumann architecture, and computer scientists knew that they could not continue to soup up the CPU indefinitely. One solution has been to spread the computing work load among multiple processors instead of channeling it through just one. Since the early 1980s, computers of very different capabilities have applied variations of this tactic, called parallel processing, to achieve greater speed. For example, the microprocessor found in many recent desktop models can assign tasks such as communications, printing, and mathematical calculations to subordinate processors, which attract the attention of their electronic overseer only when they are ready for another task. Supercomputers have evolved from having a single, powerful CPU to incorporating a pair of them, then four or more. In other machines, less capable processors are harnessed together by the dozens, the hundreds, and even the thousands to tackle huge problems Lilliputian style. One such computer, called the Connection Machine *(pages 56-59)*, contains more than 64,000 simple processors working in concert.

While some innovators sought to eliminate the von Neumann bottleneck through parallelism, others began experimenting with alternative technologies to develop new ways of computing. Some of these so-called non-von approaches are digital, some not. Some are electronic; others exploit a different medium.

Research has progressed on many fronts. Visionaries set out in the 1960s to develop optical computers, in which the photons in a beam of light would serve in place of electrons. Investigators in the field expect that even the most rudimentary optical computer will be at least ten times speedier than the fastest electronic computer. Meanwhile, other farsighted scientists took the first steps toward producing a molecular computer, whose logic circuitry might be "grown" like crystals or perhaps synthesized from living proteins. Such machines offer the potential for great speed because signals would have to travel such short distances during processing inside the computer. Applications for these devices would be manifold. On an even smaller scale are prospective devices called nanocomputers. (The term comes from nanometers, or billionths of a meter.) Hundreds of them might fit inside the nucleus of a human cell to prevent cancer or to repair damage caused by disease.

Still other non-von alternatives seek to harness the power of a holistic approach to computing: They consider all factors in a problem simultaneously rather than one at a time. The most celebrated such processor, the human brain, has provided a model for an especially promising alternative computer known as a neural network. Like the brain, a neural-network computer learns from experience, refining its performance of a given task with every repetition. Such a machine may be capable of performing the sort of "fuzzy" tasks so effortlessly managed by the human brain—understanding spoken words, reading a handwritten note, distinguishing an object from its surroundings. Fuzzy problems confound the most powerful von Neumann machine.

DIGITAL'S LONGTIME RIVAL

One alternative to von Neumann architecture predates the digital computer by centuries. Called analog devices, these calculating machines, instead of working with numbers as digital computers do, manipulate a commodity such as voltage. A simple example of the analog approach is a child's toy used to teach addition. It consists of numerals molded from plastic (the commodity) that hook onto the arms of a scale or balance. The numerals are carefully made so that each weighs according to its value. For example, a 2 and a 4 hung from one arm are balanced by the weight of a 6 suspended from the other.

In a typical analog computer, the sum of two numbers would be found by combining input voltages representing each of them, and measuring the output voltage, which represents the answer. And much as a light bulb glows the instant a switch is thrown, an analog computer offers a solution to a problem as soon as the input voltages flow through its circuits. A simple problem might be to add together the results of multiplying the numbers three, four, and seven in pairs. Mathematically, the problem is expressed as three terms to be added together: $(3 \times 4) + (4 \times 7) + (7 \times 3)$. To perform the multiplications, an analog computer would contain three circuits capable of multiplying one voltage by another. The multipliers, in turn, would be linked to an adding circuit capable of summing three voltages. The solution is a two-step process. First, voltages representing the three numbers would be applied simultaneously to the appropriate multipliers. Their output voltages would then arrive together at the adder, which would supply the answer virtually instantaneously.

A von Neumann machine working the same equation would break it down into more than two dozen steps. Just to find the product of three and four, it would store each number in memory, retrieve the numbers, multiply them together, and finally store the result, twelve. Six more steps would be required to perform each of the remaining two multiplications. Summing the products requires eight additional steps before the computer eventually arrives at the answer.

This problem is so elementary that either type of computer could solve it quickly. But if a solution required adding together the results of multiplying, say, fifty numbers in pairs—not an unusual amount of arithmetic in equations that describe electrical power grids, for example—a well-designed analog computer would have the edge in speed. The early digital computers could not even make a contest of it; they were hopelessly outstripped as they minced their way through calculations.

The price of such speed is precision; measuring a voltage can never be done as accurately as a digital computer can manipulate numbers. But analog computers excel at such applications as simulating and controlling elaborate machinery and complicated industrial processes, where the computers typically function more precisely than the objects of their attention, making digital-computer precision unnecessary. Analog computers served both the Axis powers and the Allies in World War II, and for twenty-five years afterward they vied with digital machines for a share of the burgeoning computer market, playing key roles in the design of rockets and advanced jet aircraft.

AN ANCIENT ART
Analog devices long predate the use of voltage as a calculating medium. One of the earliest was the astrolabe, an instrument for making astronomical observations and calculations; it worked by measuring and manipulating angular distances, such as the moon above the horizon. Knowledge of the principles dates from the second century BC. Probably the most familiar device to represent numbers as linear distance is the slide rule, a calculating tool that multiplies numbers indirectly by adding their exponents or logarithms and divides by subtracting them. In a simple example, 1,000 multiplied by 100 equals 100,000. The first of these numbers can be written as ten cubed, that is, ten with the

exponent three—10^3. One hundred would be 10^2, and 100,000 would be 10^5.

The slide rule, invented in England during the early 1600s, became the engineer's constant companion from the late 1800s until it was made obsolete in the latter half of the twentieth century by electronic digital calculators. Typically, the instrument consists of two equal lengths of wood, metal, or plastic, each inscribed with a logarithmic scale. A narrow piece (the slide) slips into a groove cut the length of the wider piece (the body), a design that makes it possible to add and subtract exponents—and thereby multiply and divide numbers—simply by moving the slide along the groove in the body.

Poles apart in complexity from the slide rule was an analog device called a tide predictor. Invented toward the end of the nineteenth century by the Scottish physicist Lord Kelvin, its purpose was to generate tide tables detailing the times of high and low water in various ports each day for a year into the future. Kelvin's computer depended on a then-new mathematical invention called harmonic analysis, which made it possible to derive from past tides an equation that would predict future ones. Solving the equation manually (a slide rule was not accurate enough for the purpose) took a great deal of time. To create useful tables, it had to be solved once for every hour of every day of the year—a total of 8,760 times. Even then, if high or low water fell between hours, additional calculations would be required to pinpoint the time.

Lord Kelvin's machine consisted of gears and pulleys that embodied the equation used for predicting tides. He could customize the tide predictor for most ports by altering the gear ratios and pulley positions. Solving the equation required nothing more than turning a crank that drove the gear-and-pulley mechanism and caused it to raise or lower the pen of a chart recorder. As a scroll of paper advanced through the recorder, the pen drew an undulating curve that represented the continually changing tide. As recently as the mid-1960s, the United States Coast and Geodetic Survey used a tide predictor, more elaborate than Kelvin's but based on the same idea, to calculate tides for each minute of the year with an error of less than two inches.

A MATTER OF MEGAWATTS
The seeds of the modern analog computer were sown in 1927, when an M.I.T. engineering professor named Vannevar Bush developed a machine to solve problems of electric-company power grids. These extensive networks link together the electricity-generating capacity of individual utilities to form huge wells of electrical power. Relatively new at the time and poorly understood, power grids were bedeviled by voltage fluctuations and blackouts, as enormous amounts of electricity surged from one part of a grid to another.

To fathom the networks' complex dynamics, engineers relied on differential equations—a branch of mathematics conceived independently in the seventeenth century by Isaac Newton and Gottfried Wilhelm Leibniz to analyze physical systems in flux by dividing a problem to conquer it. Each part of a problem is calculated in isolation, then the partial answers are combined to yield the full solution. Working through a set of differential equations as complicated as the ones needed to express the workings of a power grid is all but impractically time-consuming. A team of engineers might spend months working out the consequences of, say, a generator failure somewhere in the grid. Then they would devote a similar interval to examining a solution intended to prevent such an event from afflicting the entire network—and there was no certainty that the first remedy would do the job.

Bush's mechanical differential analyzer, when it was completed in 1930, automated the solution of differential equations modeling a dynamic system. Inside the analyzer, different arrangements of gears and metal shafts performed addition, subtraction, multiplication, and division. The components were linked by additional shafts. Shaft rotation signified numerical values. To represent the number 17, for example, a shaft might be rotated 17 degrees; if numbers higher than 360 were required, the rotation of the shaft could be scaled so that a movement of only 8.5, 4.25, or 2.125 degrees could stand for 17. Six integrators, ingenious shaft-driven adding devices, performed an operation in calculus called integration, the difficult linchpin of differential analysis. Bush's machine drew a solution as a curve on graph paper. In the power-grid context, the curve might peak as a spike of electrical energy blasted through the system, or it might drop suddenly to zero, indicating a power failure somewhere along the line.

Despite the complexity—and occasional mechanical balkiness—of Bush's differential analyzer, the machine could solve all manner of differential equations. A "modeler" customized the machine for each problem by linking analyzer components in an appropriate configuration; all the modeler needed was a screwdriver and a wrench. This programming often required a day or two, but once a problem had been set up, the machine could crack it in minutes.

Bush published a paper describing his differential analyzer in 1931, and the document inspired scientists in the United States, Great Britain, Germany, and the Soviet Union to build similar devices in their own laboratories. U.S. Army engineers, for example, assembled a differential analyzer at the Ballistic Research Laboratory in Aberdeen, Maryland, where in 1935 the machine began computing artillery-firing tables, which correlate range with angle of barrel elevation. Essential for accurately shooting any artillery piece, firing tables require calculations that depend not only on the type of weapon and munition and whether the target lies at a higher or lower elevation than the gun but also on the changing speed of the shell as it arcs toward the point of impact, wind speed, air temperature, and other variables. Even as Bush's machine was being cloned, he began work on a second, larger model. Upon its completion in 1942, the device was christened the Rockefeller Differential Analyzer (RDA2) in honor of its partial funding by the Rockefeller Foundation. To ease the work of tailoring the analyzer to solve a problem, Bush substituted electrical circuits for some of the cumbersome metal shafts that had linked the integrators and arithmetic units in his first machine, reducing the analyzer's setup time to five minutes or less.

WHEN CYCLOPS COMPUTED

While Bush was harnessing electricity to speed the programming of his differential analyzer, a young engineer, poet, and amateur scholar of classical Greek named George Philbrick had built a far superior machine only a few miles from Bush's lab at M.I.T. Instead of shaft rotations to represent numbers, Philbrick's computer used voltages. Completed in 1938, it was not only quick to program but, operating at the speed of electricity, it solved differential equations much faster than the spinning shafts and gears of Bush's inventions.

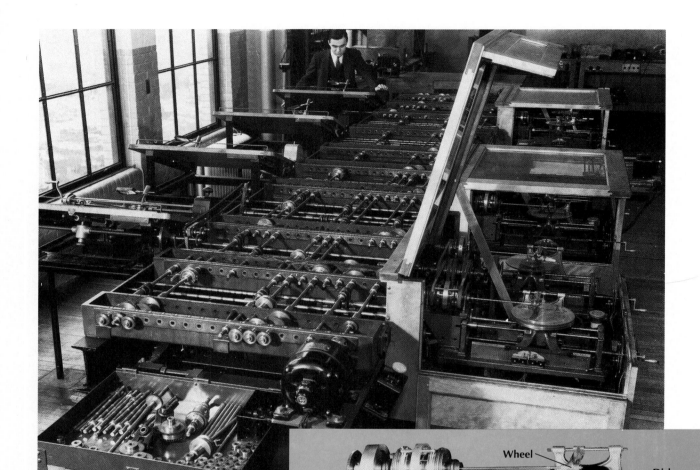

Philbrick had gone to work for a Boston instrument firm in 1935, shortly after receiving a degree in communications engineering from Harvard. Within a year, the firm merged with several others to form the Foxboro Company, which specialized in industrial process control—the technique of governing a dynamic system such as the flow of water through a turbine to generate electricity, or the purposely retarded cooling of ingots in a steel mill. Automatic control of such a process calls for quick reaction to adjust temperatures, open and close valves, count items, measure volume, and the like. Always in flux, industrial processes are, like electric power grids and the trajectories of artillery shells, best examined by differential analysis. When Foxboro asked Philbrick and engineer Clesson Mason to produce a mathematical analysis of process control in 1936, the pair embarked on a brainstorming session that led to the first all-electronic analog computer.

Enclosed in glass cases, motor-driven integrators *(above)* performed most computations in Vannevar Bush's differential analyzer. Continuously changing variables caused a horizontally mounted disk to turn at different rates. The disk rolled a small wheel, whose rotations added up to the answer.

Bush *(right)* and a colleague watch as the differential analyzer graphs the solution to a mathematical equation. The sometimes elegant curves customarily provided answers accurate within two percent.

Primarily Philbrick's creation, the computer consisted of a tall, narrow cabinet containing scores of electronic circuits. A programmer could have the computer simulate virtually any industrial process by connecting the circuits according to differential and other mathematical equations. Input voltages for factors that influenced the system (temperature, pressure, and rate of flow might be typical parameters) were supplied to the computer, whose circuitry now embodied the mathematics of the process under scrutiny. Solutions to the equations were expressed as one or more output voltages used by engineers to design controls that, under appropriate conditions, would open or close a valve, lower or raise temperature, or even bring a process to a halt. Philbrick's machine, instead of drawing a graph of the output-voltage solution on paper as Bush's computers had done, displayed the results of its computations on the circular screen of an oscilloscope. This feature inspired Philbrick to name his creation Polyphemus, after the one-eyed monster of Greek mythology.

A STARRING WARTIME ROLE

Foxboro never marketed Polyphemus; the firm regarded it primarily as an in-house analytical tool. Yet Polyphemus, which greatly streamlined the design of the company's process control systems, had demonstrated the considerable potential of all-electronic analog computers, and the machines would soon find practical application in the weapons technology of World War II.

For the Allies, an electronic analog computer appeared in the form of the M-9 gun director, used to aim antiaircraft weapons at raiding German warplanes. Shooting down an aircraft with a cannon is difficult under the best of circumstances. Even with radar, which began tracking enemy aircraft for gun crews in the late 1930s, misses were far more common than hits. Every duck hunter faces a similar problem and knows to shoot not directly at the duck, but at a point in space where the bird is expected to be in a few seconds, when the shot arrives.

The great speed of aircraft compared to ducks and the distances at which planes were engaged ruled out the hunter's practice of shooting by feel and experience. Antiaircraft gunners coped as best they could with firing tables like those prepared for other kinds of artillery and simple mechanical aiming aids, but they rarely had enough time to do a proper job of manually converting radar tracking information into a future position, then aiming the gun accordingly.

Ready for service by early 1943, the M-9 was an analog computer custom-built to calculate firing solutions for the 90-mm antiaircraft cannon. As input, the device was supplied with voltages that represented several consecutive position reports of a target aircraft. Assuming that the plane would change neither course nor speed, the M-9 constantly calculated the position the gun must assume in order for its shells to hit the target. The results were fed instantaneously to a mechanism that raised, lowered, and swiveled the gun platform, enabling the weapon to track its targets automatically even as it blasted away at them.

Rugged and reliable in the field, the M-9 proved its worth on many a battlefront. Its finest hour came during the Second Battle of Britain in 1944, when the Germans began launching pilotless V-1 jet-propelled bombs against London. In August of that year, nine out of every ten V-1s that appeared over the English Channel were blown from the sky by M-9-directed guns. During one week in particular, 90-mm batteries brought down eighty-nine of the ninety-one V-1s launched by the Germans.

OF ANALOGS AND ROCKET BOMBS
In September, the Germans unleashed a far more fearsome weapon: the supersonic V-2, a liquid-fueled ballistic missile with a range of 160 miles. Hitler's V-2 was inherently unstable in flight. Furthermore,

Soldiers manning a 90-mm antiaircraft cannon demonstrate the M-9 gun director, consisting mainly of a tracker unit (positioned directly behind the gun) and an analog computer set up to the right of the tracker. Two observers sitting in the tracker follow the target with telescopes whose movements inform the computer of the target's progress. Using this information, the computer sends electrical signals that train the gun.

in traveling so high, it passed through strong winds that could not be accurately predicted. Without a precision flight-control mechanism, the rocket might crash or drift off course in cross winds.

The answer to these control and navigation problems was an on-board electronic analog computer linked to a network of springs, weights, and gyroscopes that sensed changes in motion resulting from wind buffets or from the rocket's own flight dynamics. Any such perturbations were instantly relayed to the computer, which calculated how far the rocket was veering off course and corrected for the error by manipulating steering vanes in the tail.

The hardware for this on-board guidance system was the brainchild of an engineer named Helmut Hoelzer. He had based the prototype of the device on ideas he had formulated upon reading about Vannevar Bush's mechanical differential analyzer in 1935. Although the prototype showed great promise, firing live missiles to gauge the guidance system's performance would have been costly. To circumvent this difficulty, Hoelzer built an analog computer to simulate a V-2 rocket's flight characteristics, the first in a distinguished line of analog aircraft and missile simulators. Hoelzer's computer-generated voltages that mimicked the ones the rocket's on-board springs, weights, and gyros would produce in flight. In response, the guidance computer sent course-correction signals to the test computer, which then calculated how the rocket's guidance system had performed under the simulated conditions—and, by extension, how it might fare during actual flights.

The German rocket was immune to antiaircraft fire; it flew so fast that it was within range of the 90-mm cannon for only a few seconds before its warhead exploded, not enough time for the M-9 to aim and fire the guns at it. Nonetheless, a different analog computer—Vannevar Bush's RDA2—played a crucial role in knocking out the Germans' capacity to launch the missiles.

For nearly two years, the computer had been hard at work producing firing tables for artillery. Then one day in the autumn of 1944, the RDA2's overseer, government scientist Frank Verzuh, was asked to produce a set of ballistic tables for a projectile having an altitude and range far above and beyond those of any artillery shell he had ever heard of. He fulfilled the request, but the trajectories computed by the RDA2 were returned a few weeks later with a note saying that they were wrong. Verzuh and his colleagues at M.I.T. had apparently neglected to factor in the curvature of the earth, a crucial element in pinpointing the origin of the flight path. Verzuh ordered the tables recalculated to incorporate the new variable, then heard nothing more about the matter. Only later did he surmise that he had been asked to compute the trajectory of the dreaded V-2 as a means of targeting probable launch sites.

HALCYON DAYS ON THE ANALOG SCENE

Frank Verzuh was only one scientist whose wartime research in ballistics and fire control centered on analog computers. Another was George Philbrick, creator of Polyphemus, who had left the Foxboro Company shortly after the United States entered the war in December 1941. After hostilities ended in 1945, Philbrick elected to pursue a doctorate at M.I.T. As part of his Ph.D. thesis, he planned to design and build a fully electronic analog computer that he had envisioned during the war.

Looking beyond graduate school, Philbrick nurtured the hope of one day building analog computers for sale to companies such as Foxboro as an aid in designing their products. Precisely that opportunity presented itself in 1946, when a group of engineers from the Wright Aeronautical Corporation in Wood Ridge, New Jersey, sought out the busy graduate student. Wright's engineers, who had learned of Philbrick's wartime work, offered him $22,000 to produce an analog computer that could simulate the control system of the company's new turboprop power plant—a type of jet engine fitted with a propeller.

The jet age was not yet a decade old. The first plane powered by such an engine, Germany's Heinkel 178 prototype jet fighter, had flown only seven years earlier, in 1939, and engineers had much to learn about the new technology. Then as now, the performance of a jet engine varied widely according to the plane's speed, altitude, load, and—in the case of turboprops—propeller-blade pitch. (Set at a high pitch angle, the blades bit deeply into the air for rapid acceleration on takeoff; a lower pitch angle, which conserved fuel, was preferred for cruising.) A system designed to regulate the operation of a turboprop engine for optimum fuel efficiency would have to take all these variables into account as it adjusted the speed of the turbine or the ratio of fuel and air being mixed in the engine's combustion chamber. An analog computer, able to capture the dynamic process in the form of electronic circuits, would be ideal for modeling the turboprop's control system. By simulating the system on the computer that they hoped Philbrick would build for them, Wright Corporation engineers expected to lower the number of test flights needed to perfect their work. Money saved in the flight-test phase—which was expensive, time-consuming, and above all hazardous to pilots—would more than pay for the new computer.

Philbrick accepted Wright's proposal, even though doing so meant postponing his graduate education—forever, as it turned out. He incorporated himself as George A. Philbrick Researches (GAP/R), an electronics company that would blaze many trails in analog computing during the next two decades. Over a period of months in 1946, Philbrick and his younger brother Fred constructed the Wright Corporation's computer in a spare bedroom at his house in Cambridge, Massachusetts. The computer fully met expectations, enabling Wright engineers to significantly reduce the number of test flights. Fred, now a business partner, volunteered his garage as a place to build GAP/R's second commercial product. Its purpose was to run flight simulations for the National Advisory Committee for Aeronautics (NACA), which evolved into NASA.

Philbrick adopted a modular, or "building block," design for his computers. Individual components—each performing a mathematical function such as addition, multiplication, or integration—could be assembled to solve a wide variety of problems. Each unit had one or more input jacks and a single output jack; the computer operator chained mathematical functions together by plugging jumper wires into the jacks, linking the output of one component to the input of the next. This flexibility made possible an approach to engineering that Philbrick called "lightning empiricism." With one of his computers, an engineer could build an electronic prototype of a design within minutes of formulating mathematical expressions that described its operation. Furthermore, analog machines like those pioneered by GAP/R were naturally interactive. While the machine was operating, the user could change the parameters—that is, the constant or variable

continued on page 24

An Analog Approach to Simulation

Although the digital approach to computing has become overwhelmingly predominant, it has never been the only means for processing information by machine. For some applications, other styles of computing have proved at least equally adept. In the role of simulator, for example, the computer's job is to create an accurate model of objects, forces, conditions, or events that occur in the real world, from supersonic jet fighters in flight to the turbulent patterns of the weather. Digital computers are frequently used for simulations, but analog machines offer an alternative. These computers, which handle data in the form of continuously varying electrical signals rather than the discrete, on-off pulses of digital computers, are naturally suited to representing ever-changing phenomena.

As the name suggests, analog computers work with a stand-in—usually voltage—for the thing being computed. For every variable under study in an analog simulation—such as speed or altitude in a model of ballistic missile flight—the computer generates equivalent voltages. As a variable fluctuates, so does the corresponding voltage. As the simulation runs, variables are manipulated according to mathematical formulas that describe all the physical forces at work. Within such a computer, the formulas are embodied in special electrical components and circuitry that produce output voltages appropriate to the values of the input variables.

Simulations rely on a complex group of mathematical operations known as differential equations, which analog computers are particularly skilled at solving. In essence, a differential equation expresses how one variable changes in response to changes in others.

The following pages illustrate the basic features of an analog simulation for designing a cruise-control system to hold a car at a nearly steady speed on the highway. As shown above, these systems follow classic digital computing practice: A speed sensor on a back wheel sends an input signal to a computer, which processes the information and sends to the engine throttle the output signal appropriate for achieving or maintaining a speed set by the driver.

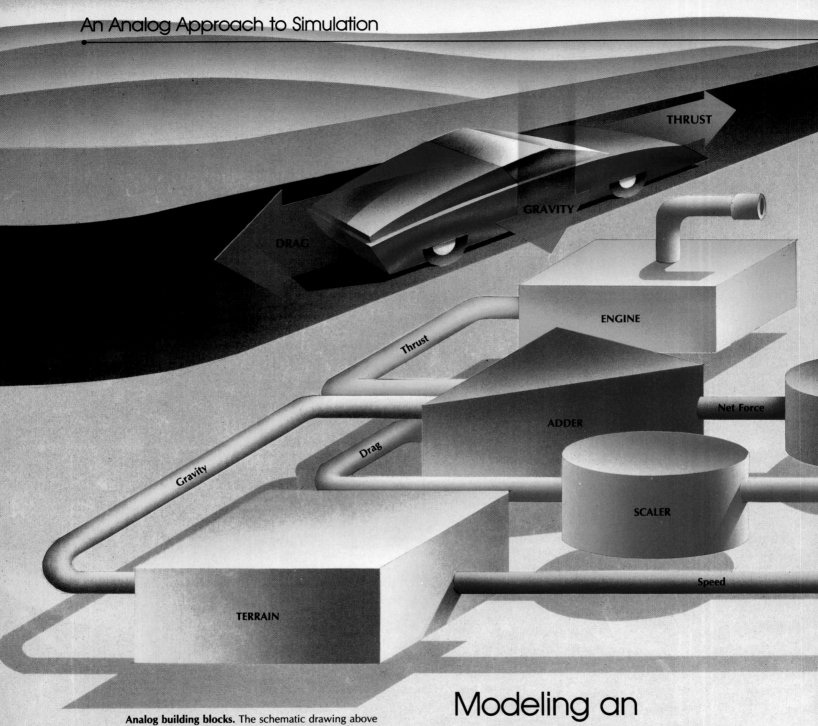

THRUST

GRAVITY

DRAG

Thrust

Gravity

Drag

ENGINE

ADDER

Net Force

SCALER

Speed

TERRAIN

Analog building blocks. The schematic drawing above depicts the relationships among the various mathematical operations an analog computer employs to simulate the effects of thrust, drag, and gravity on the speed of a car. An adder combines the three forces to produce a net force, which a scaler divides by the car's mass to determine acceleration; an integrator then uses acceleration to calculate speed *(red)*. Drag *(blue)* is computed by a squarer, which figures the wind resistance based on the speed, and a scaler, which factors in the simulated car's degree of streamlining. A set of formulas representing the terrain also uses speed to determine the car's position in a simulated landscape, then from the slope of the road at that position computes the force of gravity *(green)*. The mathematical engine model, which will eventually receive a throttle setting as input from the cruise control, determines thrust *(orange)*.

Modeling an Interplay of Forces

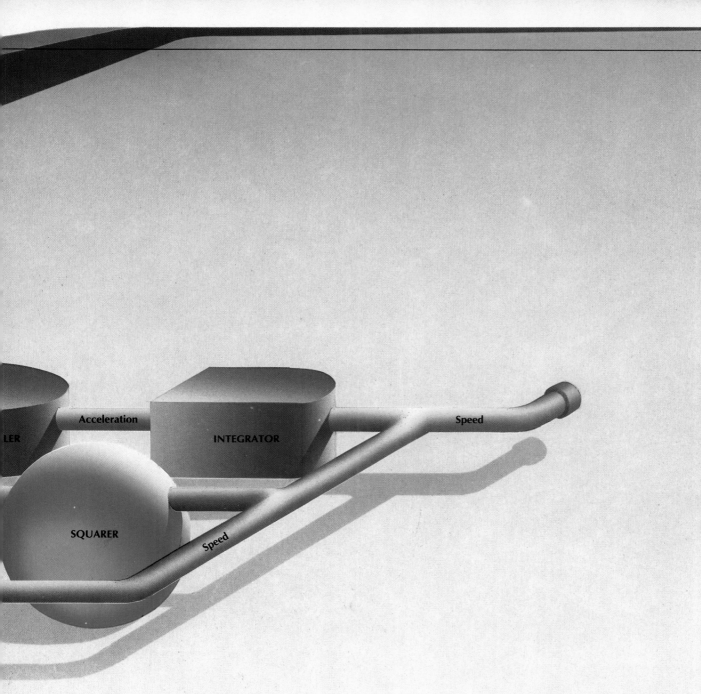

Acceleration

LER

INTEGRATOR

Speed

SQUARER

Speed

Speed

In order to generate an accurate simulation of automobile cruise control, engineers build or program an analog computer to imitate the environment in which the cruise control will operate. The speed of a car is affected by three fundamental forces, as illustrated at top: Thrust from the engine propels the car forward; drag resulting primarily from air resistance holds it back; and gravity, which constantly pulls down on the car, works either positively or negatively, depending on whether the car is moving downhill or up. A combination of components in the analog computer, each representing a specific mathematical operation, manipulates the continuously varying voltage signals that represent speed, thrust, drag, and gravitational force as they affect one another.

To solve the differential equations that govern the effects of these forces on a car's speed, an analog computer must add up all the accelerations or changes in speed that have occurred continuously over time. This operation, called integration, is enacted by a circuit called an integrator. At its heart is a relatively simple electrical component called a capacitor, an electrical reservoir that accumulates—or sums —all the fluctuations in the voltage sent to it from other parts of the computer.

As indicated in the diagram above, both the drag and gravity portions of the model form feedback loops with the central vehicle model (red), which computes speed. The next four pages illustrate two different analog versions for the cruise controller itself, which will complete the model by linking thrust as well into a loop with speed.

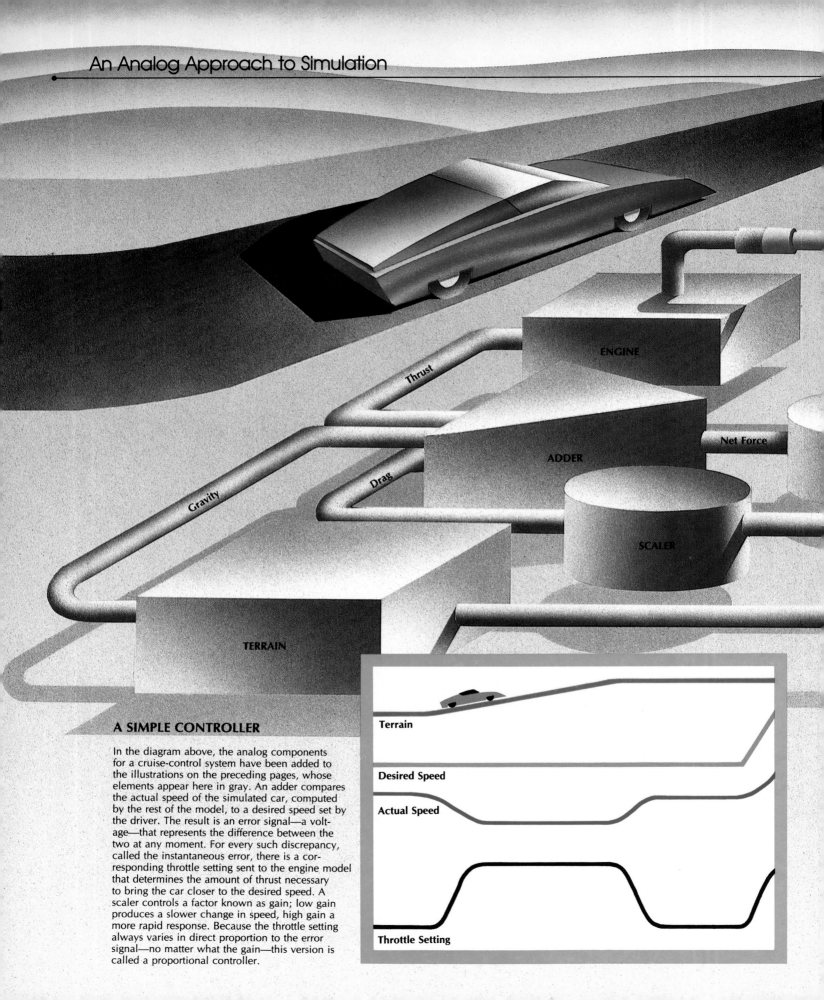

ENGINE

Thrust

Net Force

ADDER

Drag

Gravity

SCALER

TERRAIN

A SIMPLE CONTROLLER

In the diagram above, the analog components for a cruise-control system have been added to the illustrations on the preceding pages, whose elements appear here in gray. An adder compares the actual speed of the simulated car, computed by the rest of the model, to a desired speed set by the driver. The result is an error signal—a voltage—that represents the difference between the two at any moment. For every such discrepancy, called the instantaneous error, there is a corresponding throttle setting sent to the engine model that determines the amount of thrust necessary to bring the car closer to the desired speed. A scaler controls a factor known as gain; low gain produces a slower change in speed, high gain a more rapid response. Because the throttle setting always varies in direct proportion to the error signal—no matter what the gain—this version is called a proportional controller.

Terrain

Desired Speed

Actual Speed

Throttle Setting

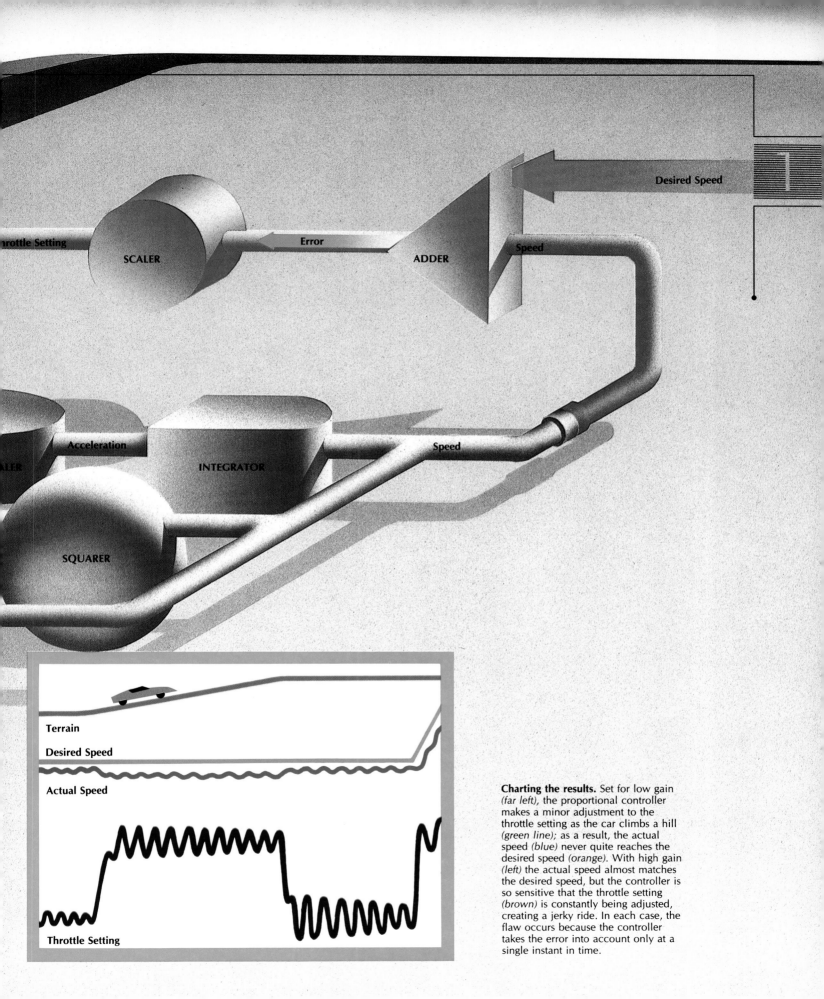

Throttle Setting

SCALER

Error

ADDER

Speed

Desired Speed

Acceleration

INTEGRATOR

Speed

...ALER

SQUARER

Terrain

Desired Speed

Actual Speed

Throttle Setting

Charting the results. Set for low gain *(far left)*, the proportional controller makes a minor adjustment to the throttle setting as the car climbs a hill *(green line);* as a result, the actual speed *(blue)* never quite reaches the desired speed *(orange)*. With high gain *(left)* the actual speed almost matches the desired speed, but the controller is so sensitive that the throttle setting *(brown)* is constantly being adjusted, creating a jerky ride. In each case, the flaw occurs because the controller takes the error into account only at a single instant in time.

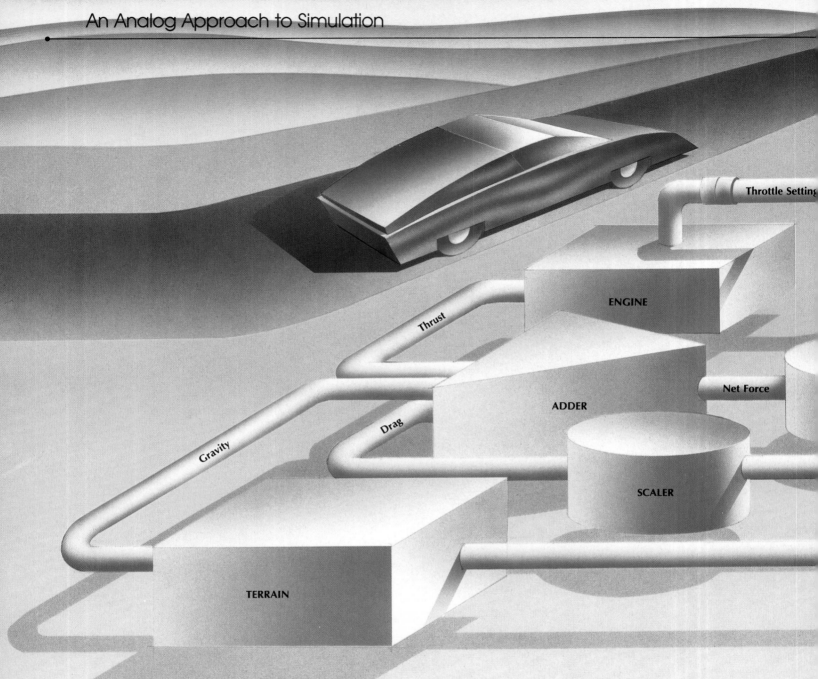

Throttle Setting

ENGINE

Thrust

Net Force

ADDER

Drag

Gravity

SCALER

TERRAIN

THE INTEGRATION ADVANTAGE

Building an integrator and a second adder into the design of the cruise control solves the problems of the proportional controller. As before, the actual speed and the desired speed are fed to an adder that continuously calculates the difference between them. Now, however, the voltage representing the instantaneous error goes through two separate processes. The integrator at the top of the diagram keeps track of instantaneous errors produced as the simulation runs, adding them together to create a cumulative error. Both the cumulative and instantaneous error signals are scaled to set the gain and then combined by another adder to yield the total error, which governs the throttle setting.

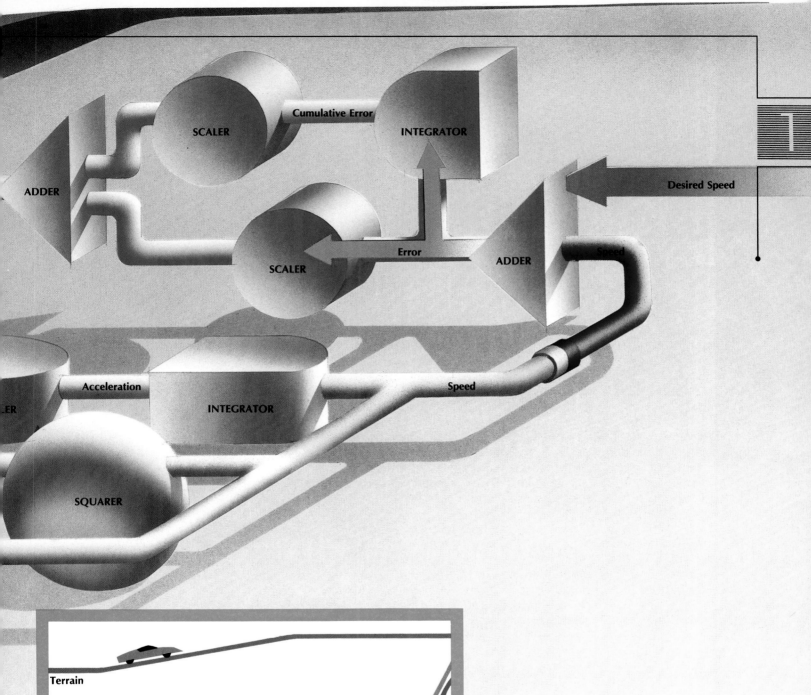

SCALER

Cumulative Error

INTEGRATOR

ADDER

Desired Speed

Error

SCALER

ADDER

Speed

Acceler...

Acceleration

INTEGRATOR

Speed

...ER

SQUARER

Terrain

Desired Speed

Actual Speed

Throttle Setting

Patterns of success. With an integrator at work, the simulation yields the intended effects. The pattern of throttle settings as the car climbs a hill to level ground shows a sensitive reaction to error without sudden or jerky adjustments. The result is a smooth and reasonably accurate match between actual and desired speeds.

terms—of the equations being solved simply by turning dials on the computer's control panel. The effects of such changes appeared instantly as an altered pattern in the solution curve flickering across the oscilloscope.

Since Vannevar Bush's day, electronic components of analog computers have suffered from a potentially devastating side effect of their own operation. Vacuum tubes, transistors, resistors, capacitors, and other electronic components have slightly different electrical characteristics at different temperatures. One consequence is that voltages in a circuit vary or drift as the components become warmer in operation. For a computer that provides voltages as solutions to problems, drift can mean the difference between correct answers and wrong ones. An imperfect remedy is to let the computer warm up thoroughly before use—a process that might take several hours—and to keep the air surrounding the machine at a constant temperature. Even then, errors can occur. Applying voltage to an electronic analog computer creates additional heat as electrons overcome the resistance (electrical friction) inherent in any electrical circuit.

Philbrick's machines were by no means exempt from drift. Indeed, GAP/R's most important contribution to analog computing was the perfection of an electronic device called a stabilized operational amplifier, or op-amp, that eased the drift problem by automatically sensing and compensating for incipient drift. From the day that Philbrick's basic op-amp model, the K2W, appeared on the market in the early 1950s, the device set the standards for low-cost precision and reliability in op-amps for a decade to come. "The K2W became the Model T of the analog world," said former M.I.T. mechanical-engineering professor Henry Paynter. "It became so closely identified with its creator that engineers dubbed it the 'phil brick.'"

FLYING BY SIMULATION

GAP/R's early work for the Wright Aeronautical Corporation presaged the growth of an analog-computing industry devoted to simulating the flight of aircraft, including ground- and air-launched missiles. Among GAP/R's closest competitors in this burgeoning arena was the Reeves Instrument Company of New York City, which had made its first analog computer under a wartime contract for the U.S. Navy. When Reeves entered the commercial market for analog machines after the war, the company remained faithful to its first customer: The Reeves Electronic Analog Computer (REAC), built in 1948, was later used to design the navy's X-13, an experimental jet that could take off vertically from the deck of an aircraft carrier. With a tall black cabinet bristling with lights and knobs, REAC struck navy scientist John McLeod as "the offspring of an illicit affair between a clothes locker and a pinball machine."

REAC and other analog computers proved invaluable in the operation of specialized machines known as flight simulators. Not only did a flight simulator help engineers design a plane and its controls, it helped teach pilots mastery of an aircraft long before the first production version rolled out of the assembly hangar. The computational quickness of the analog computer meant that the simulator could operate in "real time"—that is, events occurred in the simulator as fast as they would during an actual flight.

Numerous analog-computer manufacturers sprang up during the 1950s. Among them was a Boston firm called the GPS Instrument Company. GPS got its start in 1952 when an enterprising M.I.T. engineer named Samuel P. Giser learned that NACA was seeking a flight simulator. Giser hurriedly founded GPS and offered to build the machine for $13,000. NACA accepted Giser's bid but stipulated that the money be paid only on delivery of the machine—and that the delivery be made within just ninety days.

Giser's ready assets at the time consisted of $25 in cash and a $100 war bond. After several banks turned down his loan requests, an electronics firm in Giser's hometown of Sharon, Massachusetts, agreed to lend him the parts needed to begin construction. Working nights and weekends in an attic bedroom of his house, he completed the analog simulator by the contract deadline; to save time during the final few days, Giser's partner, Frank Spada, slept on the floor beside the machine.

GPS specialized in compressed-time simulations—computerized re-creations in which events take place more quickly than they do in reality. A flight that requires ten hours to complete in the real world, for example, might be simulated on a compressed-time analog computer in only a single hour. For scientists and engineers, such synthetic speed-up holds great appeal; it allows them to detect, in the span of perhaps a few days, failures likely to occur only after hundreds of hours of actual flight.

One of the unsuccessful bidders for the NACA contract had been a New Jersey firm named Electronic Associates, Inc. (EAI). The setback was only temporary, however, for EAI established its presence in the analog-computer field later that same year with a machine called the 16-31R, which was instrumental in the design of the reactor engine for the world's first nuclear-powered submarine, the USS *Nautilus*. EAI's analog computers were also indispensable in the design of experimental aircraft. A successor to the 16-31R, the 16-231R, formed the heart of the flight simulator for the U.S. Air Force's X-15 rocket plane, an extraordinary aircraft built in the late 1950s that could ascend to an altitude of nearly sixty miles and fly six times the speed of sound. The 16-231R's reputation for reliability was impeccable; EAI sold more than 500 of the machines to Dow Chemical and Texas Instruments, for example, making the 16-231R the best-selling large-scale analog computer in history.

THE ANALOG EDGE

Due mainly to the superior speed of analog computers (the machines could solve differential equations thousands of times faster than digital computers of the era) the 1950s and early 1960s unfolded as analog's golden age. In government laboratories, university research centers, and privately owned defense and aerospace corporations around the world, analog computers helped engineers and scientists design and analyze everything from long-distance telephone networks to fuel systems for aircraft.

Programming an analog computer—wiring together computing circuits to solve equations—had become increasingly tedious and time-consuming as the problems assigned to the machines reached a level of complexity never attempted on early machines such as Bush's RDA2. In response, both Reeves and EAI in the early 1950s developed a detachable plugboard called a patch panel. A problem could be set up on such a panel, which resembled an old-fashioned telephone switchboard, by plugging jumper wires into jacks on its face. Connectors on the back of the panel linked the jacks to the various arithmetic elements inside the computer. When the machine was needed to solve a different problem, the first patch panel was unplugged and replaced with another wired for the appropriate equations. The first program could be saved and reused later.

A MACHINE IN ECLIPSE

Although analog computers enjoyed undisputed mastery over digital machines in solving differential equations, they had traits that cast doubt on their reliability. For example, electrical characteristics of resistors, capacitors, vacuum tubes, and other electronic parts from which analog circuits were assembled changed with age. An adder having an error of 1/100th of one percent when new could, after a few months' use, begin to misbehave ten times as badly.

In computers that represented numerical values with voltages, such unpredictability was a handicap. If a voltage was off by even a small amount, the accuracy of the solution became undetectably distorted. Voltage precision was less crucial in digital machines, whose circuits represented only the binary numbers zero and one. Digital circuits could therefore tolerate a wide variance in voltages. For example, any voltage between one and three could represent a zero, while any voltage between three and five might signify a one.

Working around these impediments required taking an analog computer's pulse from time to time. One approach was to apply a known input voltage to each of the computing elements and measure the output voltage. If it was within the tolerances specified for the unit, all was well. If not, the component could be adjusted by a trimmer control that slightly changed the unit's internal resistance so that the correct voltage appeared at the output terminals. For critical applications, the computer sometimes needed to be trimmed every day.

As competition with digital computers intensified in the 1950s and 1960s, the most serious shortcoming of analog computers proved to be their lack of storage for data. Programs, of course, could be saved on patchboards, but there was no means for preserving the values of inputs or solutions to equations. Although this was a relatively minor inconvenience for engineers, it effectively prevented the use of analog computers for such tasks as keeping records or figuring a payroll—tasks at which digital computers excelled. As REAC programmer John McLeod recalled, "It was much easier to justify the cost of a computing system which could do things that the accounting department could understand than one that could only do such esoteric things as 'simulation.'" Furthermore, businesses require to-the-penny accuracy regardless of how great a sum might be at issue. An error as small as 1/100th of a percent, when applied to a million-dollar payroll, would result in a hundred-dollar error.

By about 1965, improvements in digital-computer speed and memory capacity, combined with advances in programming techniques, had made digital the technology of choice for most computer customers. Manufacturers of analog machines were left to contend for a diminishing share of computer sales, and the casualties were notable and numerous. George Philbrick sold his GAP/R to the California-based Teledyne electronics conglomerate in 1967, and Teledyne quietly phased out its line of analog machines not long thereafter. Samuel Giser, meanwhile, was forced to liquidate GPS when his bank grew concerned about the future of the analog niche in the world of computing and called in its loans. The Reeves Instrument Company, too, went out of business.

THE HYBRID COMPUTER ASCENDANT

In the aftermath of the shakeout, EAI emerged as one of the largest remaining manufacturers of analog computers, having survived by bending with the prevailing technological winds; since 1960 it had been developing a hybrid computer—part digital, part analog—that would combine advantages of both types.

In a hybrid machine, the digital computer held software that could guide an engineer in analyzing a problem, help develop equations to represent it, and specify the connections between computing components of the analog side of the machine to be established by plugging wires into patch-panel sockets. After the analog computer had been set up to solve a problem, a digital program called a checkout routine verified that no errors had been made in wiring the patch panel. The two halves of the hybrid machine communicated by means of converters that transformed the continuous analog signals into the discrete binary patterns of a digital signal and back again. Pairing the two technologies gave the analog computer access to a memory for the first time, enabling hybrid-computer users to manipulate and represent stored data in any number of ways: as numbers, as a graph, or—with the advent of sophisticated computer-graphics capabilities—as a visual representation of the physical system being simulated.

INTO THE SPACE AGE

A number of companies competed with EAI in the hybrid-computer arena. Comcor, Inc., of Denver, Colorado, for example, sold such a machine to Lockheed Aircraft in the mid-1960s, after the firm won an air-force contract to build the massive C5A military transport. The plane's designers used the computer to simulate many aspects of the aircraft's performance before it was built and to help analyze the aerodynamic qualities of prototypes in flight. In the early 1970s, NASA engineers at the Marshall Space Flight Center in Huntsville, Alabama, began using a Comcor hybrid to simulate the complexities of the fuel system for the space shuttle's main engine. The engine burns a volatile mixture of liquid hydrogen and oxygen, which must be channeled through a labyrinth of pumps, turbines, and valves before ignition in the combustion chamber. Flow of fuel—as well as the temperatures and pressures of the engine's various chambers for mixing, burning, and cooling the two elements—must be precisely controlled.

Such high-tech jobs were not enough in most cases. Comcor, like many other suppliers of analog-computing devices, eventually went out of business, its fate sealed as much by poor management as by the limited market for analog computers of any description. To survive, other companies turned away from analog devices to making digital computers.

Among the few manufacturers that held fast, none prospered more than EAI. When the company introduced its first hybrid model in 1962, NASA quickly put the machine to work. Named the HYDAC 2000 (for HYbrid Digital-Analog Computer), the device was used to simulate the system of small control rockets that maneuvered both the Mercury and Gemini space capsules. A more sophisticated successor—the HYDAC 2400—performed similar duties for the Apollo program later on. EAI computers of 1960s vintage have displayed remarkable staying power. As recently as the early 1980s, the Messerschmitt-Bölkow-Blohm aerospace company in Munich, Germany, was using a HYDAC 2000 computer to model the system of jets whose delicate thrusts—typically lasting five milliseconds or less—keep a communications satellite precisely positioned in space.

Like makers of digital computers, survivors in the analog-computer industry build their machines around microchips. When analog-computing circuits—adders, multipliers, integrators, and the like—"were vacuum-tube or discrete-transistor designs," wrote Ray Spiess of Comdyna, Inc., a competitor of EAI during the late 1970s, "these fundamental components cost hundreds of dollars. As integrated circuits, the same components cost pennies." The result: Analog computers could be designed to solve much larger and more complex problems "with an almost complete disregard for the number of components used." Gone with tubes and transistors were voltage fluctuations caused by aging circuitry.

In 1978, EAI incorporated analog microchip technology in a hybrid called the Pacer 2000 (for Precision Analog Computing Equipment, Revised). Among the customers for the computer was the Société Européene de Propulsion, a French aerospace company that relied on the machine to design the control rockets for its space probe *Giotto,* which approached within 350 miles of Halley's comet during its 1986 passage through the solar system.

FLIGHT OF THE HAWK
In 1983, EAI introduced the Simstar hybrid. With up to five times the computing capacity of the Pacer 2000, the Simstar has already proved crucial to the work of U.S. Army engineers at Redstone Arsenal, which is charged with designing and testing the control systems for all surface-to-air and surface-to-surface missiles furnished to American ground forces. Redstone Arsenal has served as the proving

ground for, among other weapons, the Hawk antiaircraft missile, one of the world's best air-defense systems.

A Hawk missile homes on its prey by means of radar echoes from an enemy aircraft. A digital, on-board guidance computer analyzes these reflections to determine the target's speed and direction, then sends commands to control fins that guide the missile toward the quarry. In a combat situation where a confusing array of aircraft, both friendly and hostile, may be crisscrossing the sky, the guidance system must keep the missile in pursuit of its intended target and not permit it to home on another aircraft. The computer must also filter out electronic "noise," such as jamming signals, and if the target is flying low to the ground, the system must be able to ignore "ground clutter," errant radar signals that carom off the terrain below the target.

Using a Simstar, Redstone engineers create on the ground the conditions likely to confront a Hawk in the air. Simulations take place in a large chamber equipped at one end with a "target array" bristling with 550 radar antennas. At the opposite end of the chamber, pointed at the array, sits a missile mounted on a motor-driven flight table—a platform that moves the missile about its three flight axes: pitch, roll, and yaw.

Every step of the simulation, which is designed to reveal how a missile would perform in combat, is choreographed by the Simstar. As the target array emits signals mimicking radar echoes from an enemy aircraft attempting to evade the missile, the signals are received and analyzed by the on-board guid-

ance computer, which then issues commands that in actual flight would be flashed directly to the missile's control surfaces. In the simulation, they go instead to control surfaces simulated in the Simstar, which translates them into flight-table movements.

By controlling emissions from the target array, the Simstar can constantly vary the conditions of the experiment—introducing decoy targets or jamming signals, for example—and monitor the missile's response in real time. The Simstar can also represent changing environmental factors such as cross winds and air density, which affect flight performance. Test data recorded in the memory of the Simstar's digital component are analyzed later to determine whether the missile hit or missed its simulated target.

Engineers term such experiments "hardware-in-the-loop" simulations because an actual device—in this case, the Hawk guidance system—rather than a mathematical or computer model is put to the test. Hardware-in-the-loop simulation saves the time and expense of creating such a model, which at best can only closely approximate the operation of the real thing. Moreover, this practice enables engineers to test guidance systems for a fraction of the cost of firing a live missile and monitoring its actual performance (the price tag attached to a single test shot can be as high as $1 million). In 1986, army designers made such effective use of the Simstar to design a modification of the Hawk's guidance system that a single test flight—rather than the eight or more customary in the past—was needed to demonstrate that the missile was ready for production.

THE ANALOG HORIZON

NASA will soon receive a Simstar computer to replace its aging Comcor machine. Unable to find a digital machine that can match a hybrid's speed at any practical cost, the agency has remained faithful to hybrid computers, as have many other research-and-development groups. Paul Landauer, chief system architect at EAI, estimates that "there must be 300 hybrid labs in operation around the world. Many of them have recently been updated, and a lot of younger people are learning the technology. They're discovering that, in comparison with the very abstract and artificial way in which a digital computer works, the hybrid approach approximates much more closely the real-world system being simulated."

But the future is by no means secure. Many computer-industry analysts believe that hybrid computers will soon join their purely analog forebears in an extinction brought on by the ever-growing speed, power, and memory capacity of digital machines at ever-declining cost. An expert who holds this opinion is Robert Howe. Now a professor of aerospace engineering at the University of Michigan, Howe in 1957 founded Applied Dynamics International (ADI) to make analog computers. ADI was among the companies that ultimately abandoned the business to build digital computers. "Most simulation," notes Howe, "is done all digitally, including missile simulation." In his view, the handful of companies that continue to build analog or hybrid computers are living on borrowed time. Perhaps Howe and the others are right about analog and hybrid computers that work electronically, but alternatives are under investigation. It is more than possible that analog computing will resurge in the very different realm of light (Chapter 3).

Neural-Network Strategies

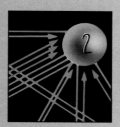

Despite half a century's development, the digital computer has yet to match the information-processing faculties of a three-year-old child. Tasks easily mastered by a preschooler—learning to pronounce everyday words, for example, or recalling an entire memory when prompted with just a fragment or two—have eluded conventional machines and their step-by-step manipulations of precise data. Inspired by the superiority of the human brain at processing "fuzzy" information, a handful of psychologists, neuroscientists, and computer experts have designed an alternative architecture known as the neural network.

A neural network is a web of densely interconnected processing elements, called neurons or nodes for their functional resemblance to the basic nerve cells of the human brain. Like their biological counterparts, the neurons in a neural network can send information to—and receive information from—thousands of fellow processors at once.

The links by which the neurons communicate are critical. Each interconnection—called a synapse after its neurological equivalent—can be assigned a positive or negative value, allowing some neurons to excite responses in their connected processors and others to inhibit them. The strength of every synapse can also be modified, or weighted, to control the intensity of the signals passing from one neuron to the next. This arrangement enables the network to arrive at collective decisions based on the exchange of information among its many processors.

In special-purpose neural networks—those dedicated, for example, to a specific group of tasks known as optimization problems *(pages 36-39)*—the pattern of connections is set in advance by the designer. In other, more flexible networks, the connections change in response to the magnitude or frequency of the signals being transmitted among the neurons. Such adaptability, characteristic of neural nets, enables a network to "learn" a task by performing it repeatedly.

Three types of neural-network architecture—one designed to learn by example, a second devoted to problem solving, and a third capable of memory by association—are examined on the pages that follow.

Teaching a Machine to Speak Up

The three-tiered architecture of NETtalk, a neural net that has been trained to read English text out loud, typifies the design of networks that learn by example. Two key features make the network a capable student. The first is the inclusion of a middle layer of neurons between an input layer and an output layer. Because it is difficult to attribute the network's overall results to individual neurons, the middle layer is often called the hidden layer. Neural networks equipped with a hidden layer enjoy a degree of superiority over two-layer systems comparable to that of the thinking brain over the reflexive spinal cord: They can be trained to perform complex tasks —pronouncing letters differently according to their context in a word, for example—that remain beyond the grasp of any two-layer net.

The second feature that enables this type of neural net to learn is a technique known as the backward-error-propagation algorithm, or back propagation for short. Whenever the network mistakenly identifies a given input, the algorithm measures the severity of the error—that is, it computes the disparity between the network's output and an ideal output as defined by the network's designer—and propagates an error code backward through the system. As the error message travels from output layer to hidden layer to input layer, the links that channeled the incorrect signals through the network are weakened in strength—that is, their synaptic weights are lowered. This has the effect of reinforcing the interconnections that are likely to produce a more accurate response upon the network's next try.

In NETtalk, this structure and method combine to yield a neural net capable of converting strings of written characters into phonemes, or the discrete parts of speech. The phonemes in turn drive an electronic voice synthesizer. The back-propagation algorithm need be iterated only a few times before the system begins to produce intelligible sounds. How NETtalk—and other trainable neural nets like it—accomplishes this anthropomorphic feat is shown at right and on pages 34 and 35.

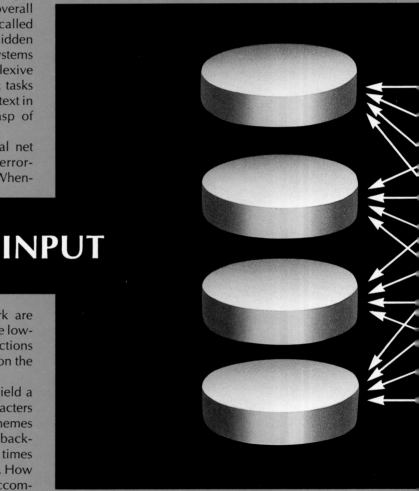

INPUT

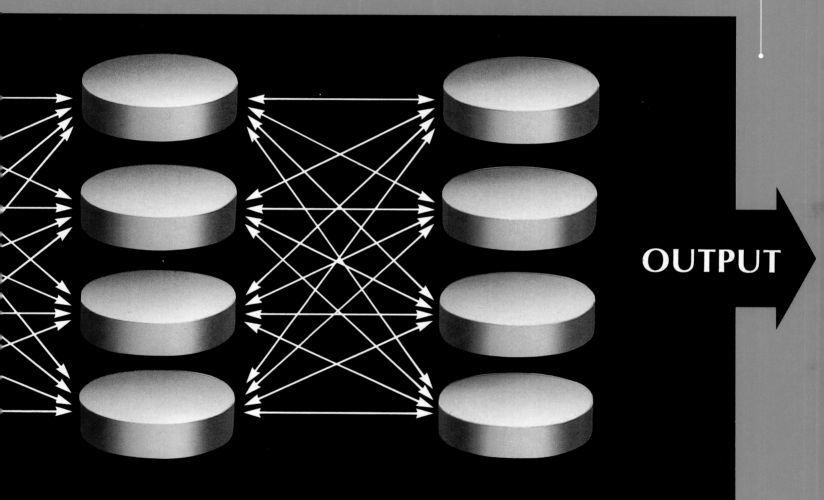

OUTPUT

A blueprint for learning. This network, designed for learning, consists of three layers of neurons. Every neuron in the input layer *(above, left)* is linked to every neuron in the middle, or hidden, layer *(above)*. Similarly, every hidden-layer neuron connects to every neuron in the final, or output, layer *(above, right)*. The interconnection strengths, or synaptic weights, can be adjusted incrementally by the network's learning algorithm, which combs backward through the net to modify the intensity with which each neuron affects its partners in the layers adjacent. Actual learning systems contain many more neurons than appear in this schematic model. In NETtalk, for example, the input layer contains 203 neurons, the hidden layer 80, and the output layer 26, making for 18,629 synaptic connections in all.

A Trial-and-Error Learning Process

Before a neural net can be trained to master a task, the link between every pair of neurons in the network must be assigned a small random weight. This seemingly arbitrary step, known as random initialization, is necessary for establishing a point of departure from which the network can converge on a correct solution. As a result, the network's first attempt to classify an input is nothing more than a wild guess.

In the case of NETtalk, for example, the network's initial try at pronouncing the written letter *n* might yield the sound *ah*. This leaves considerable room for improvement through a process of trial and error. The neural net invokes its learning algorithm, which compares the output with a predefined standard (in NETtalk, a phonetic transcription of a person reading the letter *n*) and begins adjusting the network's connection strengths to reconcile the actual with the ideal. These piecemeal refinements might eventually lead the network to come up with the sound *em,* for example; from there only a few extra adjustments would be required to arrive at the proper pronunciation of *en*.

The algorithm works its corrective magic until the network's designer determines that further changes in the connection strengths will bring about only negligible improvements in the system's performance. In one ten-hour training period, for instance, NETtalk learned to pronounce 1,000 sample English sentences with 95 percent accuracy; to increase that figure appreciably would have required another ten-hour tutorial session.

A shot in the dark. In the neural network's first stab at identifying an input, all interconnections are assigned random weights. The input—shown at right as a pattern of active and inactive neurons in the input layer—triggers a chance configuration of hidden-layer neurons to emit signals of their own. (Signals propagated forward through the network are depicted as green arrows, whose thickness denotes the weight of the link that carries them; for clarity, only one hidden-layer neuron has been activated here.) The signals from the hidden layer then trip neurons in the output layer, whose on-off pattern represents a guess rather than the correct response.

Fine-tuning the weights. The back-propagation algorithm judges the degree of error between the network's actual and ideal outputs (at right, the second neuron in the output layer has been corrected from "off" to "on"), then adjusts the synaptic weights to reduce that disparity. As a first step in propagating the error code backward through the network, the output-layer neurons representing the correct answer send signals *(purple arrows)* that alter the links to the hidden-layer neurons. These modify the connections to the input-layer neurons, weakening the links that produced the wrong answer and strengthening those that will contribute to the right one on the next try.

Trying again. As the give-and-take of back propagation begins anew, the input-layer neurons transmit marginally corrected signals to processors in the neighboring hidden layer. In the chain of events at right, the topmost neuron in the input layer has been trained to send an attenuated signal to the hidden layer, which in turn fires strong pulses to the output-layer neurons it is beginning to recognize as the proper ones. After many such training cycles, the network begins to consistently produce the correct pattern of outputs.

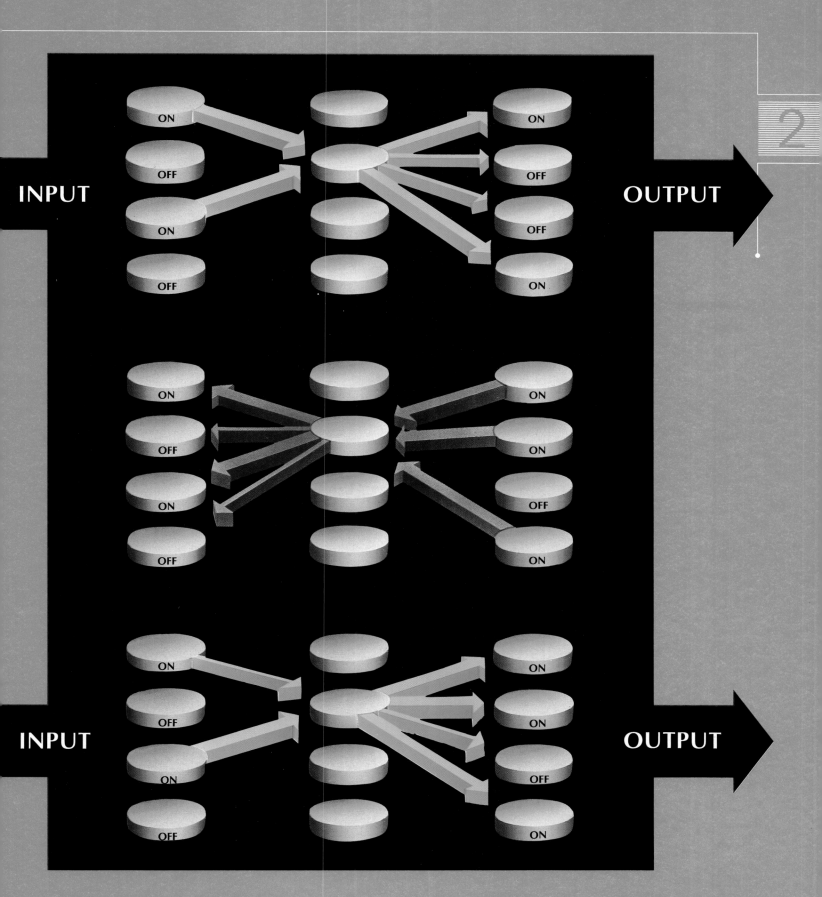

In Search of the Best Solution

A second type of neural network, named the Hopfield net after its designer, John Hopfield, specializes in optimization problems—knotty conundrums whose solution lies in the optimum combination of a huge number of interacting variables. In a task-assignment optimization problem, for example, the goal is to apportion a variety of tasks among a group of people whose skill at each task differs widely. To find the best mix of jobs for only six people, a serial computer could quickly calculate and compare all 720 possible arrangements. Instructed to perform a similar allotment for fifteen people, however, the machine would be faced with more than 1.3 trillion alternatives—a formidable undertaking even for a supercomputer.

The Hopfield net can master optimization problems twice

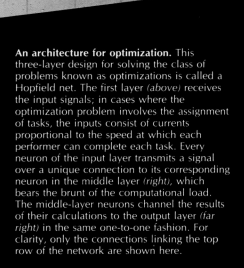

An architecture for optimization. This three-layer design for solving the class of problems known as optimizations is called a Hopfield net. The first layer *(above)* receives the input signals; in cases where the optimization problem involves the assignment of tasks, the inputs consist of currents proportional to the speed at which each performer can complete each task. Every neuron of the input layer transmits a signal over a unique connection to its corresponding neuron in the middle layer *(right)*, which bears the brunt of the computational load. The middle-layer neurons channel the results of their calculations to the output layer *(far right)* in the same one-to-one fashion. For clarity, only the connections linking the top row of the network are shown here.

that big in less than a microsecond. The speed-up stems from the unique architecture of the net, which is designed to recognize that the optimal assignment of each person hinges on the work rate of every other person. The net's input layer is a squared array of neurons, in which each column represents a worker and each row represents a job to which he or she will ultimately be assigned. The input-layer neurons receive data in the form of voltages proportional to the rate at which each worker can complete a given task, then feed this data forward in one-to-one connections to neurons in the middle layer.

Because only one worker can be assigned to each task, only one neuron in each row and column will be allowed to emerge triumphant in the end. Inhibitory links therefore connect each middle-layer neuron to all the processing elements in its particular row and column. These connections carry signals whose negative strength serves to dampen the intensity of weaker competitors. Each middle-layer neuron totals the effect of these mutual exchanges and feeds the resulting signals forward to the output layer, where the pulses are displayed as lighted squares on a grid. This routine is repeated until one neuron in each row and column emerges as the dominant one, and the pattern of winning neurons represents the optimum solution to the problem.

How such a design might enable the Hopfield net to perform a specific optimization problem—assigning six reporters with varied skills to the beats that will yield the most stories for the group as a whole—is illustrated overleaf.

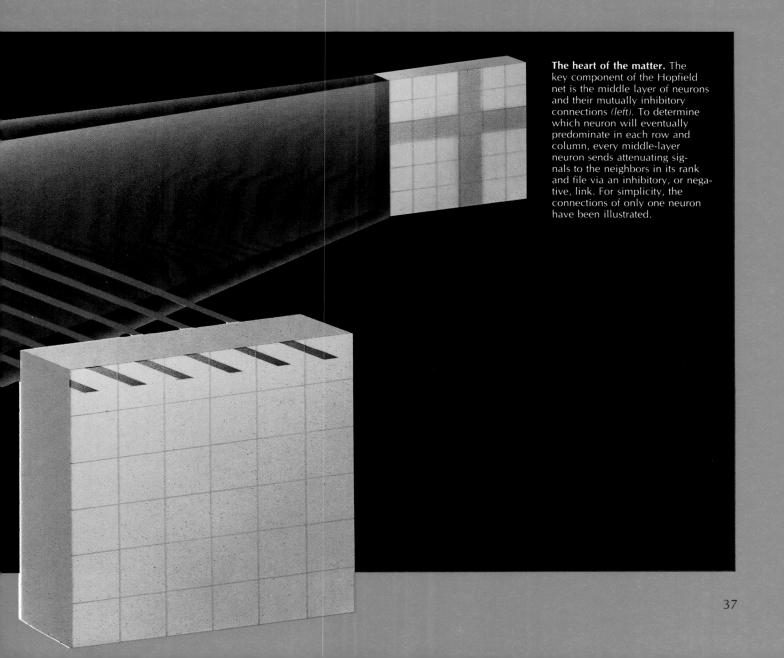

The heart of the matter. The key component of the Hopfield net is the middle layer of neurons and their mutually inhibitory connections *(left)*. To determine which neuron will eventually predominate in each row and column, every middle-layer neuron sends attenuating signals to the neighbors in its rank and file via an inhibitory, or negative, link. For simplicity, the connections of only one neuron have been illustrated.

5	3	4	9	4	7
3	1	10	6	7	5
6	6	6	7	5	2
7	6	1	2	2	4
2	8	5	4	6	3
7	4	6	3	3	2

37	28	29	37	30	35
28	26	36	32	34	32
32	32	32	34	37	27
36	34	26	28	28	31
27	36	31	30	33	29
35	30	33	29	29	28

5	3	4	9	4	7
3	1	10	6	7	5
6	6	6	7	5	2
7	6	1	2	2	4
2	8	5	4	6	3
7	4	6	3	3	2

5	3	2	191	9	82
2	7	346	5	24	9
23	24	12	46	42	15
109	34	2	6	14	35
4	195	4	1	49	12
113	12	15	9	25	17

And may the strongest neuron win. This three-stage sequence represents the multiple iterations that a Hopfield net performs in solving the editor's task-assignment problem. As shown in the first progression above, the input-layer neurons receive voltages proportional to the work rates from the table opposite, then feed these signals forward to corresponding middle-layer neurons. Each neuron in the middle layer generates a negative version of this signal and broadcasts it as an inhibitory pulse to every other neuron in its row and column. These exchanges cause marginal differentiation of the middle-layer neurons, as shown by the values above. The leading neurons at the end of this first round are displayed in the output layer, where neurons vie for supremacy in rows 1 and 2.

As signals continue to course through the net, the contention in row 2 is resolved, but row 1 remains congested (middle sequence, right). Further iterations (opposite) cause a single neuron in each column to approach the highest value, while the other values dwindle to negligible amounts, rounded off to zero. The best solution, indicated by the pattern of activated output neurons, involves some local inefficiency: Kris is the fastest arts writer, but Rick gets that beat for the common good.

itor's dilemma. Before the Hopfield
gins its attack on the newspaper
s task-assignment problem, the data is
ed in a table as shown at right. The
ns indicate the number of stories each
r can write per week for the news
ries listed in the rows. The editor's
o assign each reporter to the category
ll result in the highest output for the
overall—is an optimization problem
se the best solution requires all
es to interact. Converted into
tionate voltages, the numbers will
as inputs for the first layer of the
ld net, whose problem-solving
que is illustrated at left and below.

	KRIS	PAUL	ANN	SEAN	PAT	RICK
NATIONAL NEWS	5	3	4	9	4	7
LOCAL NEWS	3	1	10	6	7	5
SPORTS	6	6	6	7	5	2
ARTS	7	6	1	2	2	4
EDITORIALS	2	8	5	4	6	3
BUSINESS	7	4	6	3	3	2

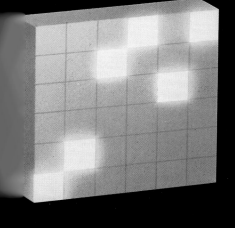

5	3	4	9	4	7
3	1	10	6	7	5
6	6	6	7	5	2
7	6	1	2	2	4
2	8	5	4	6	3
7	4	6	3	3	2

000	000	000	999	000	000
000	000	999	000	000	000
000	000	000	000	999	000
000	000	000	000	000	999
000	999	000	000	000	000
999	000	000	000	000	000

Memory by Association

Like a person conjuring up scenes from the past when reminded of just a few details, a third variety of neural network can retrieve entire chunks of information at the slightest prompting. This humanlike trait, dubbed associative memory because the items of data are stored and recalled in association with one another, makes neural nets especially attractive for applications that demand the processing of incomplete or ill-defined inputs: An associative-memory neural network might create an image of an aircraft, for example, on the basis of fragmentary radar returns showing just 10 to 20 percent of the plane's total profile.

In contrast to a conventional computer, where bits of data are lodged in individual memory cells, an associative memory distributes its information among the network's many neurons and their interconnections. This makes the network's performance independent of specific clusters of neurons; when individual processing elements fail, the system as a whole exhibits what is termed graceful degradation—that is, its operation drops off gradually rather than crashing to an abrupt halt.

The number of pieces of information required to set an associative memory in motion is typically the square root of the size of the memory being sought after. Ten facts, for example, suffice to call forth a memory made up of 100 facts. And although many distinct memories can be superimposed in a single network, their number is generally limited to 15 or 20 percent of the total number of neurons in the net; a network of 200 neurons would therefore have a capacity of thirty to forty discrete memories.

How data are encoded and then stored in an associative-memory neural network is shown below and at right; the process of jogging the network's memory is illustrated on pages 42 and 43, where the goal is to recover an entire six-fact memory when only half of it is known.

FEATURES ASSIGNED TO NEURONS

	1 SEX	2 AGE	3 INCOME	4 EDUCATION	5 MARITAL STATUS	6 EMPLOYMENT
-1	MALE	UNDER 35	30,000+	HIGH SCHOOL	SINGLE	SKILLED
+1	FEMALE	OVER 35	-30,000	COLLEGE	MARRIED	UNSKILLED

Converting memories into patterns. To endow a demographic database with the power of associative memory, statistics such as sex, age, income, education, marital status, and employment are first differentiated by the values +1 and -1 (above). These positive and negative values are then arranged in a table (right) that captures the individual characteristics of a variety of people. The pattern of positive and negative signals (green and orange squares), shows that Diana, for example, is a single woman over thirty-five with a high-school education; she earns less than $30,000 at a skilled job.

NEURONS

	1	2	3	4	5	6
DIANA	+1	+1	+1	-1	-1	-1
MARY	+1	-1	+1	+1	-1	+1
FLORA	+1	+1	-1	+1	-1	-1

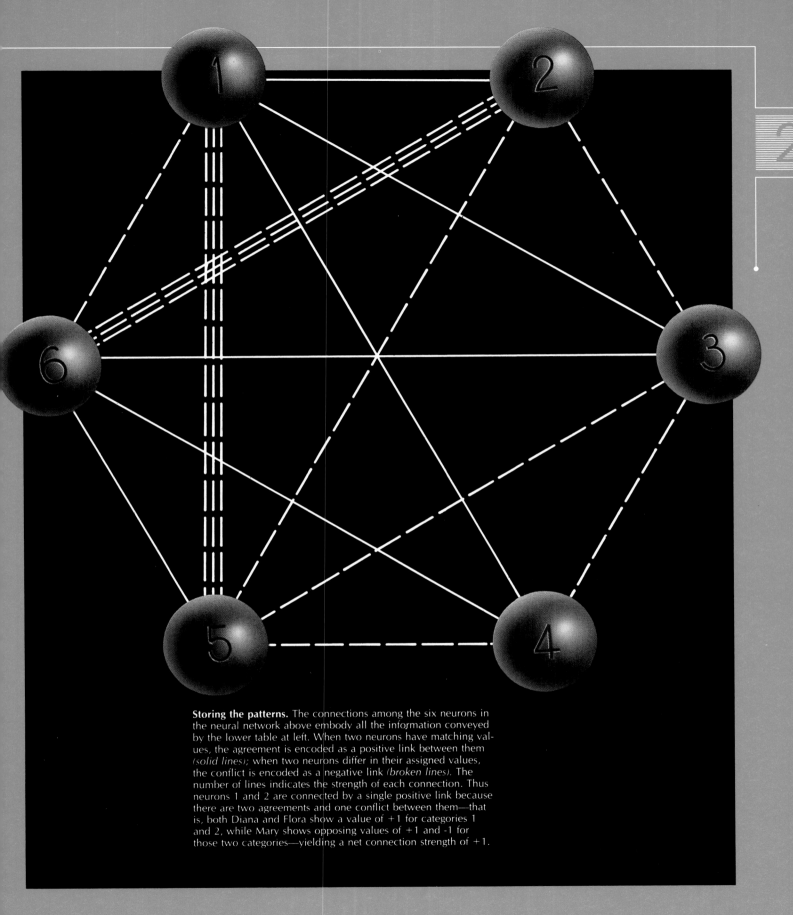

Storing the patterns. The connections among the six neurons in the neural network above embody all the information conveyed by the lower table at left. When two neurons have matching values, the agreement is encoded as a positive link between them *(solid lines)*; when two neurons differ in their assigned values, the conflict is encoded as a negative link *(broken lines)*. The number of lines indicates the strength of each connection. Thus neurons 1 and 2 are connected by a single positive link because there are two agreements and one conflict between them—that is, both Diana and Flora show a value of +1 for categories 1 and 2, while Mary shows opposing values of +1 and -1 for those two categories—yielding a net connection strength of +1.

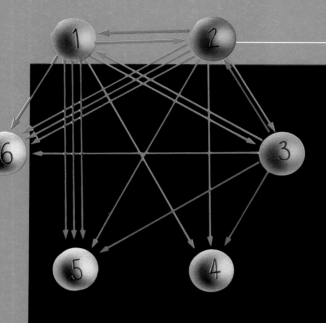

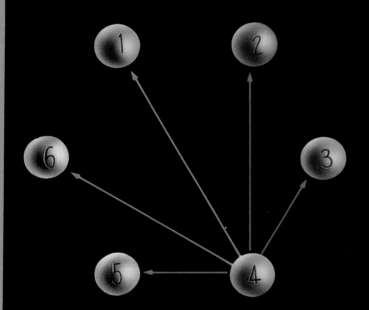

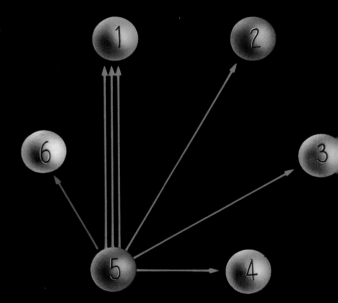

Jogging the network's memory. To identify a person on the basis of a partial description, the network is set in motion by entering all known data. In the sequence that begins at left, the three facts available—the individual is a woman, under thirty-five, and earns less than $30,000—are lodged in the network by assigning to neurons 1, 2, and 3 the values dictated by the table on page 40: Neurons 1 and 3 are set to positive values *(green)*, while neuron 2 is set to a negative value *(orange)*. These values activate the network, causing data to spread throughout it; neuron 2, for example, sends its negative signal over the existing negative link to neuron 4, a combination that generates a positive input *(green arrow)* to neuron 4.

Identifying neuron 4. In random fashion, a neuron whose value remains unknown—here, neuron 4—is selected to tally its inputs. Along with the positive signal it receives from neuron 2, neuron 4 receives a second positive signal from neuron 1 and a negative signal from neuron 3; neuron 4 thus takes on a net positive value. With its identity established, neuron 4 can participate in the associative-memory process by emitting output signals of its own. Its links to neurons 1 and 6 are positive, so those two neurons each receive a positive signal *(green arrows)* from neuron 4; by the same token, the negative connections linking neuron 4 to the other neurons in the network cause neurons 2, 3, and 5 to receive negative signals.

Neuron 5 joins the fray. Revealing the identity of neuron 5—one of two neurons whose value remains unknown—begins with a summing of the neuron's inputs. Although neuron 1 is positive, its three negative links to neuron 5 dictate that it send a signal with a value of -3 to neuron 5. Neuron 2 fires a negative signal over its negative link, resulting in a positive input to neuron 5; neurons 3 and 4, though both positive, send negative signals by virtue of their negative links. With neuron 5 receiving five negative signals and only one positive signal, its net input is negative. The influence of neuron 5 on its fellow memory elements can now be calculated, as shown above.

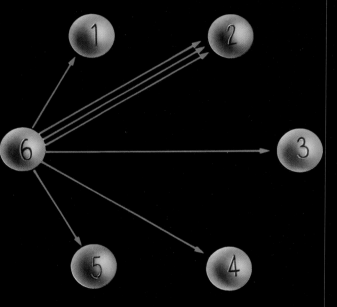

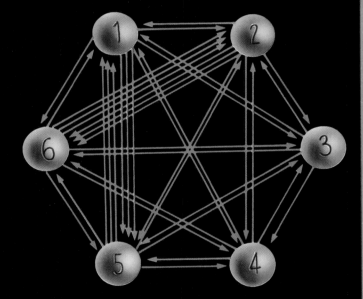

Neuron 6 revealed. The value of neuron 6—
the last memory element to be queried—is
determined by the same process of aggregating
the signals it receives from the other neurons.
Neurons 1 and 5 contribute negative inputs, but
2, 3, and 4 all send positive signals; the identity
of neuron 6 is therefore revealed to be a positive value. Activated by this electronic interro-
gation, neuron 6 sends a single negative signal
to neuron 1, a triple negative signal to neuron
2, and positive signals to neurons 3, 4, and 5.

Forging the missing links. With all six of its
memory elements active, the neural network
settles into a stable state—that is, no more
changes will occur because the value of each
neuron now reflects the sum of all its possible
inputs. The final pattern *(above)* shows neurons
2 and 5 to be negative and the others positive.
This configuration is then compared with the
table of personal statistics on page 40, whose
second row of positive and negative values
matches the pattern here; the network has filled
in the sketchy data it first received to reveal
that the partial description referred to Mary.

Stalking the
Electronic Brain

In a laboratory at the University of Pennsylvania not long ago, radar expert Nabil Farhat fed his computer some fragmentary radar returns showing just 20 percent of the sinogram, or radar profile, of an unidentified airborne target. Within seconds, Farhat's computer had fetched a complete image of the plane from its data store, and the screen before him displayed the label and unmistakable profile of a B-52B bomber—swept wings, forward-slung engines, and all. A similar technology was at work in a laboratory in Providence, Rhode Island, where a researcher scribbled letters of the alphabet on a touch-sensitive pad. As he wrote, the same letters showed up in an orderly typeface on a computer screen before him. And at a third laboratory in Baltimore, Maryland, the room filled with the clipped diction of words and sentences being enunciated by a computer learning to read English text out loud.

This trio of feats—recalling whole images from partial information, recognizing handwritten characters, and converting written words into spoken—was accomplished by a new and extraordinarily promising breed of computers, dubbed neural networks for their brainlike architecture. A neural net consists of a multitude of neuronlike processors arrayed in a vast interconnected web. Information is stored not as bits of data in individual memory cells, but as the strengths and patterns of interconnections among neurons. Nor is this information confined to binary digits: The links between neurons can assume a wide range of values, including fractional numbers such as .03 or 2.75. And in a final departure from conventional operation, neural networks do not follow rules written in a computer program; instead, they "learn" to perform tasks by being shown a series of examples.

This computational strategy makes networks fast, but it is a speed that comes at the expense of precision. A neural net is ill-suited, for example, to performing the sort of straightforward mathematical calculations at which digital computers excel. When psychologist James A. Anderson of Brown University used a neural network to perform simple multiplication in 1988, he found that "It did fine—if your idea of an acceptable answer is '7 times 5 is 40ish.' Otherwise, it did a terrible job."

Despite their imprecision, neural networks boast an uncanny—and highly prized—ability to spot patterns in mounds of data. This trait has persuaded many psychologists, physicists, and computer scientists that neural networks may someday vault the highest hurdles of artificial intelligence: understanding human speech, recognizing objects visually, and making intuitive guesses based on incomplete data.

Neural-network research exploded in the 1980s as government laboratories, corporations, and universities in the United States, Europe, and Japan launched programs to study the new brainlike computer designs. The United States Department of Defense earmarked tens of millions of dollars for an exploration of how neural networks might help the armed services to identify

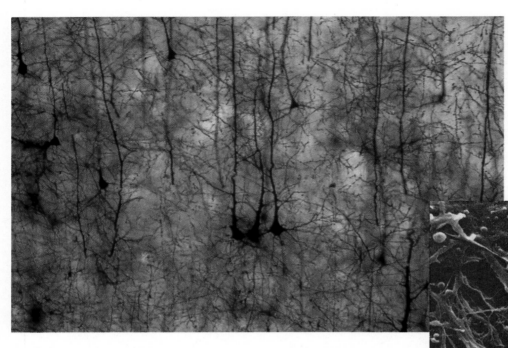

Dyed orange for clarity, brain tissue seen through an ordinary microscope appears as a maze of nerve cells, each with a long shaft called an axon and numerous tendrils that link one cell to another. Nerve-cell bodies, which contain the cell nuclei, are shown as dark spots. When magnified 500 times by a scanning electron microscope, the spots become bulbous shapes set into a seeming rat's nest of links between neurons (below).

and track targets with greater speed and reliability. Proclaiming that "The technology we are about to embark upon is more important than the atom bomb," Jasper Lupo of the Defense Advanced Research Projects Agency (DARPA) in 1988 announced his agency's intention of building a neural network with 10 billion interconnections. It was a lofty goal, and a distant one; the most sophisticated neural network of the day, although it contained several thousand neurons, took the form of a software simulation that ran on a digital computer. And even if DARPA reaches its faraway objective, a neural net of 10 billion links would have the neural complexity of only an insect. "I hope by the end of this we'll be up to a bee," said Lupo.

While the military pursued networks that could detect an approaching enemy, private enterprise embraced the devices for their money-making potential. In 1986, only two or three companies were attempting to market neural nets, but by decade's end the ranks had swelled to more than fifty. Having glimpsed the power of neural nets to endow computers with humanlike faculties, commercial firms put networks to a number of imaginative uses: reading numbers and verifying signatures on checks, controlling assembly-line robots, taking dictation, even processing applications for credit cards and mortgages.

Forward-thinkers in the academic community, meanwhile, focused less on the engineering obstacles to be overcome than on the contributions the neural-net approach might make in advancing pure science. About 100 large-scale research programs totaling $20 million are under way at major universities across the United States and Canada, notably Brown, Caltech, Carnegie-Mellon, Stanford, the University of California at San Diego, the University of Colorado, the University of Southern California, and the University of Toronto. Investigators at these institutions have set out to answer some tough questions: Are neural networks really models of the human brain? And what insights into the mysteries of neurobiology or the human mind might a study of such devices yield?

For all its futuristic appeal, the idea of arranging neurons in a computing network is nothing new. Neural networks galvanized scores of researchers in the 1950s, soared in promise and popularity during the 1960s, then plummeted into obscurity during the 1970s. In the 1980s, they sparked renewed interest in alternative-computer designs of all sorts. As those fluctuating fortunes suggest, the sociology of science has played almost as large a role in shaping neural networks as has the quest to translate an inspired idea into a working device.

TOWARD A MACHINE WHO THINKS

The groundwork for the neural networks of the late 1980s was laid in the early 1940s. Contemplating the automatic calculating machines Enigma and Purple that the Allies had used to decipher complex enemy codes during World War II, many engineers speculated that the devices could be pushed a step further to perform such advanced tasks as reasoning, problem solving, and perhaps even understanding language and visual scenes.

The first glimmerings that this hunch might be correct came from brain researchers of the day. In 1943, Warren McCulloch, a research psychiatrist at the University of Illinois, joined forces with an eighteen-year-old Harvard mathematics student named Walter Pitts to formulate a theory of how the brain's billions of neurons, or nerve cells, might give rise to rational thought. Such a cell, suggested McCulloch and Pitts in a scholarly paper, can be likened to a binary electronic circuit: The neuron can assume either of two stable states, depending on the strength of the signals it receives through its synapses, or connections, with other neurons. When the various signals equal or exceed a fixed threshold, the two men posited, the neuron is active; when the signals fall short of that threshold, the neuron remains dormant. By functioning as a simple threshold-logic device, the neuron can thus represent the true or false propositions that form the basis of logical thought.

Actual neurons, neurophysiologists have since discovered, are far more complex than those envisioned by McCulloch and Pitts—for one thing, they respond to inputs in a graded, rather than simply on-off, fashion—yet the theoretical reverberations of the McCulloch-Pitts paper echo to this day. The paper's central finding: that simple elements, when yoked together in a network, can yield extraordinary computing power.

With its promise of complexity arising from simplicity, the McCulloch-Pitts neuron inspired a generation of psychologists and computer scien-

tists to attempt capturing the sophistication of the mind in the circuitry of a machine. Further inspiration came from a book titled *The Organization of Behavior,* written by Donald Hebb in 1949. The chancellor of McGill University in Montreal and a psychologist by training, Hebb suggested that for the brain to learn a new concept or task, some physiological change must occur inside it. Specifically, he proposed, the simultaneous activity of two connected nerve cells would strengthen the link between them. If signals emitted by neuron A repeatedly prompt a neighboring neuron B to issue signals of its own, Hebb wrote, "some growth process or metabolic change takes place in one or both cells such that A's efficiency, as one of the cells firing B, is increased." On subsequent activations, he concluded, the reinforced connection between the two neurons would allow A to excite B more readily; the more often A and B were activated at the same time, the stronger the connection between them would grow.

ENTER THE PERCEPTRON

Hebb's concept of reinforcement among neurons became the cornerstone of techniques developed in the 1950s that enabled neural networks to recognize specific patterns. The chief architect of these methods was Frank Rosenblatt, who had attended the Bronx High School of Science with a young man named Marvin Minsky. Minsky later cofounded the subdiscipline of computer science known as artificial intelligence, which challenged—and very nearly eclipsed—the neural-network approach that became Rosenblatt's lifework.

After earning a bachelor's degree in social psychology in 1950 and a doctorate in experimental psychopathology in 1956, Rosenblatt joined Cornell University's Cognitive Systems Laboratory in 1958. There, he designed his first neural network and named it a perceptron to herald its apparent powers of perception.

Immense fanfare attended the perceptron's unveiling. The physicist and prominent science writer Jeremy Bernstein, for one, called the device "a remarkable machine, capable of what amounts to original thought." Yet the perceptron was at first only an incorporeal creation. Seeking to avoid the cost and complexity of hand-wiring together the hundreds of electronic components needed to form a neural circuit, Rosenblatt instead chose to simulate, or model, the perceptron's operation on an IBM 704 mainframe computer. Most neural-net researchers since then have taken the same approach, programming a digital computer to re-create network behavior. The programs simulate interneural connections and their weights as a matrix of interconnected numbers, performing exactly the same way a hardware version would—but far more slowly.

Like most of its successors, the IBM 704 that hosted the perceptron's simulation was a serial machine, processing its data one step at a time and in sequence. This method was ill-suited to the architecture of a neural network, where information is distributed among hundreds or thousands of individual processors operating simultaneously. The digital simulation therefore took nearly half an hour to synthesize processes that the perceptron, with all its neurons performing their computations at once, could have sped through in a fraction of a second—had but a circuit-board or chip version of the perceptron existed.

The simulated perceptron could classify several different visual patterns, such as very simple triangles and squares; it could also distinguish among certain letters of the alphabet. These results convinced Rosenblatt that his approach to mimicking the mind was the correct one. "As an analog of the biological brain," he wrote in 1959, "the perceptron seems to come closer than any system previously proposed."

The simulation's success emboldened Rosenblatt to cross the line from software to hardware, and in 1959 he and a group of laboratory coworkers painstakingly constructed a working version of the perceptron. The device was made up of components that acted like McCulloch-Pitts neurons and followed Hebb's rule—"Links between neurons grow stronger with use." The Mark I, as Rosenblatt called the network, featured an input layer containing 400 photoreceptors, or light-sensitive devices, roughly modeled after the neurons in the retina of the human eye. Each receptor measured the light reflected from a small part of the machine's field of vision and translated the intensity of this light into electrical signals; the pulses were then sent to the perceptron's second layer, which consisted of 512 neuron-like devices known as associator units, or A-units.

Faithful to the prevailing neurological wisdom of the day, which held that the brain's neurons are interconnected arbitrarily, Rosenblatt wired the A-units to the photocells in an entirely random pattern, with every A-unit linked to a maximum of about forty input cells. Each A-unit added up the signals it received from the input neurons and compared the result to a predetermined threshold value. When the total matched or exceeded the threshold, the A-unit—true to McCulloch and Pitts's design—fired a signal to one of eight response units, or R-units, in the perceptron's third layer; when the total failed to meet the threshold, the A-unit simply remained quiet. Finally, the R-units summed up the signals they had received from the various A-units and classified the input pattern as belonging to one of eight possible categories. It was this last step that caused a letter under scrutiny to be identified as, say, an *A* rather than an *H*.

In order to put Hebb's rule into practice, Rosenblatt devised a means of modifying the strength of the Mark I's interconnections. He attached a motor-driven resistor—an electronic component that governs the amount of current flowing from one point to another in a circuit—to every wire linking the A-units to the R-units. (Connections between the A-units and the retina, though arbitrary, were fixed; they therefore contained no resistors.) The resistors could be set to high or low values;

a high value would mean a weak connection, since the passage of the current between two neurons would be largely blocked, whereas a low value would yield a strong connection.

Rosenblatt then presented a series of training patterns to the perceptron. Whenever the perceptron correctly classified an input pattern, the value of the resistors was kept the same; whenever it incorrectly classified a pattern, the resistors between the neurons responsible for producing the wrong response were raised in value, inhibiting their signals. The device thus behaved like an overcritical teacher, as Marvin Minsky characterized it: "With perceptrons, one never rewards success; one only punishes failure." After being shown a dozen or more training patterns, and with the strength of its connections modified each time, the Mark I could "learn" to recognize a limited number of simple patterns. This faculty gave the perceptron the capacity to generalize: Drawing on its exposure to earlier, similar patterns, the Mark I could correctly sort patterns—a handwritten letter rather than a typeset character of the alphabet, for example—that it had never before encountered.

Frank Rosenblatt, designer of the perceptron, had great ambitions for his neural-network computer—even to launching it on autonomous explorations of space. Once asked what might lie beyond his invention's ken, he replied: "Love. Hope. Despair."

Because the perceptron's resistors were driven by motors, the device made a pleasant whirring noise as it learned. Despite such melodious operation, the perceptron displayed some discordant behavior. For one thing, patterns that appeared against unfamiliar backgrounds tended to foil its attempts to classify them. For another, the workings of the Mark I resisted analysis; Rosenblatt was unable to explain exactly how his creation arrived at most of its results.

Still, the Mark I's potential for "complex adaptive behavior"—that is, for learning from experience—was enough to spur some engineers into designing neural nets of their own. Just a few months after Rosenblatt unveiled the operational version of his perceptron, Stanford University electrical-engineering professor Bernard Widrow teamed up with his graduate student Ted Hoff (the man who would later build Intel's first microprocessor, the 4004) to assemble a neural network called ADALINE, for ADAptive LInear NEuron. ADALINE's design drew heavily on that of the Mark I, but it featured a built-in procedure that was designed to improve the computer's performance automatically and continuously, not just when the system had incorrectly classified a pattern. Because ADALINE was constantly striving to reduce errors, it became immediately useful for a wide range of practical engineering applications.

In its first such day-to-day use, ADALINE was put to work producing adaptive filters, which "clean up" the echoes on telephone lines. Such echoes arise from the chaotic voltage fluctuations that accompany changes in the volume and routing of calls. Adaptive filters also proved crucial to the later development of adaptive equalizers, which do everything from blocking radar-jamming signals to curtailing the number of errors in computer data transmitted by phone.

Expert-system champion Marvin Minsky, Rosenblatt's chief nemesis in the 1960s on the subject of perceptrons, later regretted the chilling effect of his book *Perceptrons* on neural-net research. Yet Minsky maintains that his purpose was to elucidate, not to cause mischief. "I am not the devil," he said to an audience of scientists in 1988.

ADALINE, the Mark I, and a handful of machines like them generated intense excitement in the computer-science community of the early 1960s. Indeed, by midpoint in the decade an estimated 1,000 researchers were investigating various neural-network designs. But with the hope came hyperbole: Proclaiming the superiority of perceptrons to the conventional computers of the day, Frank Rosenblatt announced that his device had "established beyond doubt" its ability to perform "human cognitive functions at a level far beyond that which can be achieved through present-day automatons." It was an odd claim to be made by the man who had pioneered the simulation of perceptrons on such "present-day automatons" as the digital computer, and it would embroil Rosenblatt in an academic debate of unusually high acrimony.

CRASH GOES THE PERCEPTRON
In particular, Rosenblatt's claims vexed researchers in artificial intelligence, who felt that the quickest route to their goal of a "thinking machine" lay in the manipulation of high-order symbols by a digital computer following a program of logical rules. Two champions of this viewpoint were Marvin Minsky and Seymour Papert, the codirectors of M.I.T.'s Artificial Intelligence Laboratory. As Minsky and Papert saw it, neural nets were shunting talented researchers and precious grant money onto an isolated siding of computer research. The two men therefore believed, remarked Jeremy Bernstein, that establishing the perceptron's limitations was "a sort of social service they could perform for the artificial-intelligence community."

In 1969, Minsky and Papert published the results of a four-year-long study of perceptrons. Incorporating some precise and elegant mathematical proofs, their book *Perceptrons* spelled out just what could and could not be done by a two-layer neural network—that is, a system with a single set of adjustable connections, such as those between the A- and R-units in Rosenblatt's Mark I. They showed, for example, that two-layer nets could not determine whether a graphic pattern had been drawn with a single connected line or with two or three broken ones.

This inability to compute connectedness was a severe failing, wrote Minsky and Papert, because it excluded the perceptron from a class of very simple logic devices that can determine whether a curve is in one piece or in several. A logic device such as a simple automaton can perform this operation by moving along the surface of the curve, first in one direction and then the other, until it reaches the ends; the presence of any unreachable portions of the curve beyond those two ends betray that the curve is not connected.

Minsky and Papert also demonstrated—convincingly so, it appeared at the time—that a straightforward and important logic operation called exclusive OR (X-OR) would forever elude the perceptron's abilities. The X-OR operation requires a computing element such as a switch to turn on when either of its inputs is positive, but to remain off when both of its inputs are positive.

To be sure, Rosenblatt had freely acknowledged many of the perceptron's limitations: The perceptron, he had conceded in a paper introducing the device, was literal, inflexible, and ill-equipped to handle abstractions—qualities that made it behave something like a brain-damaged patient. Nonetheless, the Minsky-Papert book delivered a near-knockout punch to the field of neural networks. Faced with a choice between neural-net research, which by the late 1960s had produced no tangible advances beyond Bernard Widrow's adaptive filters, and with developing AI programs for digital computers that were growing more powerful by the day, most computer scientists abandoned their work on neural nets. In a telling sign of the networks' fall from academic grace, Widrow and his colleague Ted Hoff arranged to drop all mention of neurons from the acronym ADALINE; where ADALINE had once stood for ADAptive LInear NEuron, it now came to mean ADAptive LINear Element.

The crowning blow came in the summer of 1971, when the field of neural networks lost its most impassioned crusader. While sailing on the Chesapeake Bay with two students from Cornell University, Frank Rosenblatt was swept over the side of his sloop, the *Shearwater,* and drowned.

MODELS OF THE MIND

Throughout the 1970s, researchers investigating neural networks led the academic version of a hardscrabble existence, constantly casting about for the meager grant monies available. Despite the lack of backers, a few scientists continued to explore the possibility that neural nets might break some hallowed computational molds. Psychologists especially remained interested in the field, because their discipline stood to benefit enormously from any light that neural nets might shed on the mechanics of brain functions. Indeed, the human mind itself cannot meet the high standards that Minsky and Papert had held the perceptron to: Psychologist James Anderson has pointed out that anyone looking at the two spirals adorning the cover of the book *Perceptrons*—one drawn with a single line, the other drawn with two—would be unable to tell which one was connected without tracing their contours by hand. This suggested that human beings and the perceptron shared some of the same computational limitations.

The allegiance of the neural-net faithful would be amply repaid as network models began to exhibit behavior far beyond the reach of traditional machines. Perhaps the most useful of these exotic traits was associative memory—the ability of a network to recall entire parcels of stored information when prompted with just a few constituent fragments. The brain displays precisely this type of memory: A refrain from an old song, for example, can trigger all sorts of associated memories—whom you first heard the song with, what you ate or drank as the music played, where you were at the time. Associative memory reverses the customary pattern of a digital computer's memory searches, which take longer to complete the more data there is to rummage through. Neural-net researcher Stephen Grossberg of Boston University pointed out the sort of thing that would happen if the brain worked this way: "As you grew older and had more faces in your memory, it would take you longer to recognize your parents."

Grossberg belonged to the small group of researchers who remained enthusiastic about neural nets during the 1970s. In 1976 he developed a neural network capable of creating categories and sorting objects among them. Together with Gail Carpenter, a professor at Boston's Northeastern University, Grossberg later unveiled a successor version, called Adaptive Resonance Theory 2 (ART 2), that correctly organized forty different images of trucks—some reduced in size, others rotated or turned upside down—into four groups. The accomplishment was notable because Carpenter and Grossberg had provided ART 2 with no predefined categories at the beginning of the exercise. It was therefore up to the system to group the trucks in categories that the network itself had identified as being representative of more than one vehicle.

A system like ART 2 might come in handy in any number of situations. Besides the obvious military applications—distinguishing enemy tanks from those of friendly forces, for example—ART 2 would give unique powers to, say, a robot exploring the ocean floor. Whenever the automaton encountered an unfamiliar seabed obstacle, ART 2 could create a new category to classify the image, and at the same time alert the robot's controllers on the surface that it had come across something worth a closer look.

NEURAL NETS RESURGENT

Following their near eclipse in the 1970s, neural networks began to strongly influence the course of alternative-computer research in the 1980s. Advances in the speed, power, and economy of operation of digital computers had made it easier for researchers to simulate new and more-sophisticated neural-net designs on conventional machines. And just as the neural-net camp had suffered from its failure to produce concrete results in the 1960s, so too did critics now begin to fault AI's slowness in fulfilling its potential. For example, no AI program had come close to mastering such tasks as understanding human speech or recognizing visual images.

One man in particular would reignite interest in neural-network computers. He was John Hopfield, a physicist at Caltech who had received his Ph.D. from Cornell in the same year—1958—that Frank Rosenblatt was there polishing up his theories about the perceptron. Hopfield had gone on to do experimental research in solid-state physics at AT&T Bell Laboratories.

Hopfield possessed a scientific curiosity that frequently drove him to explore fields of inquiry bordering his own. In the late 1970s, for example, one of Hopfield's students at Princeton University, Terrence J. Sejnowski, had started Hopfield thinking about how groups of neurons in the brain might process their information. How is it, Sejnowski asked Hopfield, that biological neurons able to transmit only about 100 impulses per second are able to retrieve stored memories so much faster than computer-memory circuits operating at one million times that speed?

Hopfield eventually found an analogy in physics. In 1982 he proposed that a network of neurons, like any other physical system, always seeks out its lowest possible energy level. Later he used a landscape metaphor to spell out what he meant. Whenever a memory is stored in a neural network, it transforms the energy of the net into a unique pattern of peaks and valleys. Each memory stored in a net can be thought of as possessing its own location in the landscape, with the memories lying at or near the bottoms of the valleys. In a process Hopfield likened to a raindrop trickling downhill, the network fetches a stored memory by settling into the computational energy level, or pattern, that most closely resembles the input data it has been asked to match.

The originality of Hopfield's analysis helped bring neural networks to the attention of engineers and computer scientists the world over. Before Hopfield's arrival on the scene, said Brown University's Anderson, many computer researchers and other practitioners of

Physicist John Hopfield, shown here against the projected image of neurons from a cat's brain, rehabilitated neural networks after the decade of neglect that followed Minsky's book. Early inspiration came from the nervous system of the common garden slug.

54

the "hard" sciences had tended to overlook the contributions of psychologists exploring neural networks because "psychologists are 'squishy.' A Caltech physicist, though, is impressive." And persuasive, too, he might have added; Hopfield delivered a number of inspiring lectures all over the globe from 1983 to 1985. Partly as a result, hundreds of bright researchers—including many physicists who had shied away from neural networks and their social-science aroma—now entered the field.

A HIDDEN PROMISE

A number of additional theoretical breakthroughs have since suggested that the Minsky-Papert epitaph for neural networks was, like the reports of Mark Twain's death, "greatly exaggerated." *Perceptrons'* authors, after dismissing the potential of two-layer networks, had speculated that three-layer neural nets would be similarly hobbled: "We consider it important to elucidate our intuitive judgment," wrote Minsky and Papert in 1969, "that the extension to [multilayer systems] is sterile."

Still, the three-layer neural network shone as a bright theoretical beacon for many scientists during the 1970s and 1980s because it promised computational powers equivalent to those of the brain over the spinal cord. With signals passing through an intermediate layer "hidden" between its input and output neurons, a three-tiered network would be able to perform a wider range of operations on the data those signals represented. Perhaps the most important operation was the ability to ferret out potentially significant statistical regularities; such patterns are often veiled by inconsistencies that can blind conventional computers to their existence. "Hidden layers," as a leading physicist in the field put it, "can detect broad classes of features of things that are present in the input data."

Yet this increase in cognitive power brought with it an extra dimension of complexity. Because hidden-layer neurons influence a network's input and output in ways that are hard to pinpoint, they remained a "black box" to network designers charged with specifying the connection strengths between the middle-layer neurons and their counterparts in the input and output layers.

Salvation came in the form of a self-correcting algorithm, or step-by-step mathematical procedure, known as backward error propagation. Back propagation or back prop, as it is called, evolved from the labors of several researchers working individually and in concert over a period of nearly twenty years. The earliest framer of the algorithm was Paul Werbos, who had earned a bachelor's degree in economics at Harvard in 1967. Like Hopfield and his interdisciplinary voyaging, Werbos was drawn to investigate a number of domains outside his specialty. In 1968, for example, he suggested that certain intuitions in psychology—specifically, Sigmund Freud's conjecture that learning occurs when energy is propagated through the brain cells in a direction opposite to that of electrical pulses—might translate smoothly into mathematics.

Fulfilling his own prophecy, Werbos developed a rudimentary back-propagation algorithm in 1971 that incorporated just this notion. Werbos's algorithm was later refined by computer scientist Geoffrey Hinton and psychologists David Rumelhart and Ronald Williams. In an experiment conducted at the University of California at San Diego in 1985, the trio proved that a neural network armed with a more elaborate version of Werbos's algorithm could

The complete system. In this schematic view of the Connection Machine and its cast of supporters, four standard computers *(orange)* prepare programs for parallel execution. A switching device called the Nexus *(red)* relays programs to the four quadrants of the Connection Machine proper *(blue)*. In each one, a sequencer *(green)* organizes program steps for assignment to the processors. Besides internal memory resources of 512 megabytes, the Connection Machine has an external data vault of ten billion bytes *(purple)*.

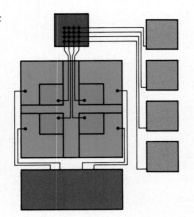

Cubes of computing power. Measuring just over five feet on a side, the Connection Machine *(below)* is divided into eight sections separated by air gaps for cooling the computer. Each of the eight cubes is a card cage holding sixteen vertically aligned circuit boards *(right)*. These are linked to display lights visible on an outer face of the cube, which facilitate the pinpointing of malfunctioning components and other hardware problems.

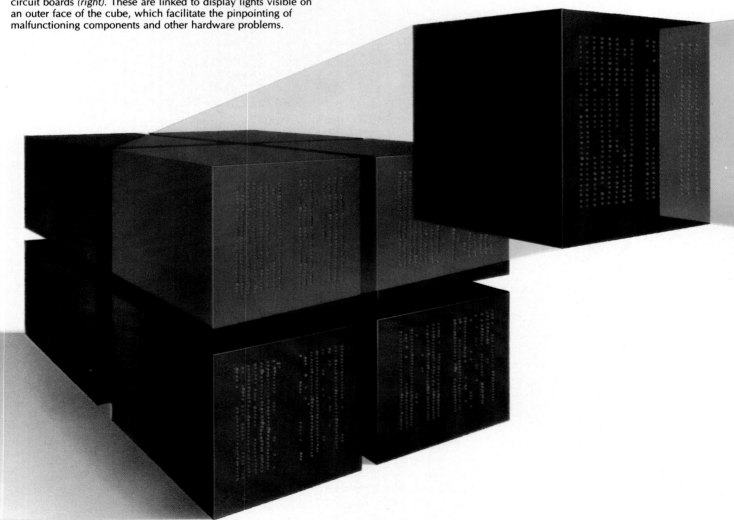

2

Just as a single-lane road can handle only a fraction of the traffic of a multilane thruway, the power of conventional computers is inevitably limited by their sequential approach to processing, in which a single processor works on problems one step at a time. To overcome this classic bottleneck, designers are exploiting a processing strategy known as parallel computing, in which many processors work simultaneously on different parts of a problem. Among the innovative hardware designs developed for this new way of computing is the Connection Machine, a massively parallel computer that links together 65,536 separate processors.

The Connection Machine excels at problems requiring relatively simple calculations on large amounts of data because each data element can be assigned to its own processor. Making a contour map from a stereoscopic pair of photographs of terrain, for example, involves routine computations comparing thousands of equivalent picture elements, or pixels, in each photograph. A sequential computer performs these simple comparisons over and over again, laboriously working its way through the job. With the Connection Machine, however, all of the pixel data can be fed to separate processors and the entire image processed at once.

As explained here and on the next two pages, an intricate organizational structure is the key to the Connection Machine's ability to coordinate its vast array of computing resources for maximum efficiency.

Processor-packed chips. Each of the Connection Machine's 128 circuit boards contains thirty-two chips *(above)*, for a total of 4,096 chips. Etched on the surface of every chip *(right)* are sixteen processors *(black)*, each with its own small memory *(white)*. A communication channel called a router *(yellow)* allows direct connections between any pair of processors on that chip and with other routers. The Connection Machine devotes a relatively large fraction of a chip's area to processing; in traditional computers, more than 90 percent of a chip is used for memory.

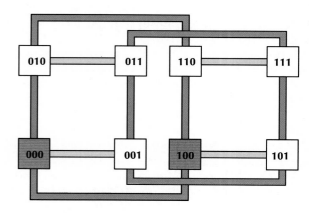

Communication between routers is illustrated here and at right in a small system of eight routers, each of which is identified by a three-bit address. Router 000 is looking for a path to router 111. It begins by comparing the first bit of the goal address *(left)* with the first bit of the three routers to which it is connected. Finding a match, it chooses the line leading to router 100 *(above)*.

Making All the Right Connections

Even though the heart of parallel processing is the simultaneous execution of independent portions of a program, processors in a parallel system must be able to work together if they are to have any appreciable collective force. Programs often depend on processors being able to keep track of the actions of other processors or to share their results; in studies of the motions of fluids, for example, processors handling the computations for individual molecules must take into account the effect of other molecules, handled by other processors. The secret to the Connection Machine's success is an efficient system of connections that allows any two of its more than 65,000 processors to exchange information.

Since every processor is connected to a router, the question is how to link up the routers. The most logical approach would seem to be direct connections between every pair of routers, but with 4,096 routers, the Connection Machine would need more than eight million wires. A simple chain of connections from one router to the next is also inadequate because communications between processors at opposite ends of the chain would be unacceptably slow.

In the solution employed by the Connection Machine, each router—identified by a twelve-bit address—is connected in a special pattern to twelve others with related addresses, forming altogether a vast network of interconnected routers. Using fewer than 25,000 wires, this design guarantees that no message ever has to travel over more than twelve wires. The schematic representations on these pages for simplified systems of eight *(above)* and sixteen *(right)* routers demonstrate how router addresses help to guide the flow of communications.

The wiring pattern itself ingeniously avoids delays by providing several equally short pathways between any two routers. Thus even if many links in the system are temporarily busy, an efficient route is usually still available.

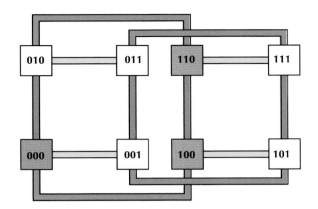

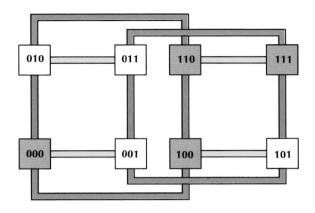

The next step is to examine the second bit of the goal—again a 1—and find a path from the current router, 100, to a router with a second-bit value of 1. Two of the paths from router 100 lead to routers having 0 as the second bit of their addresses, but the third path links to router 110.

In the final step, the third bit of the goal address is compared with the addresses of the three routers connected to 110, one of which is the goal itself. The three-step route shown here from 000 to 111 is only one of several equally short routes that could have been chosen. Had router 100 been busy, the address comparison could have switched to the second bit, and a path through 010 and either 110 or 011 selected instead.

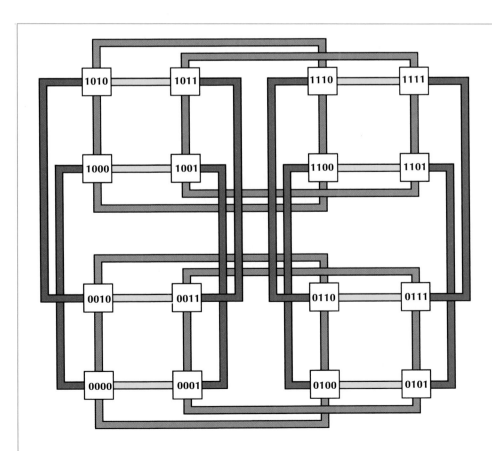

A Web of Sixteen Routers

The same communication strategy described above is easily extended to a larger number of routers with only a minimal increase in delay. At left, two systems of eight routers each are linked into a single sixteen-router network through eight new connections (red) between comparably positioned routers in the two systems. In this larger network, each router needs an address of four bits and is connected to four other routers instead of three. With the addition of only one more step in the finding of a path, each router has access to eight more routers than it did in the smaller network.

distinguish whether a given pattern contained an odd or an even number of elements. The algorithm thus gave neural networks the ability to compute parity, which happens to be a generalized case of the X-OR operation. Traditional digital computers and modems had long since mastered the task as part of their error-correction schemes, which compute parity to detect the presence of extraneous data bits.

Like a patient teacher, the back-propagation algorithm trains a neural net to perform a certain operation by repeatedly guiding the net through it. The connection strengths are initially set to small, random values ranging between, say, -.3 and +.3. The network is then given an input, and the neurons produce a stab-in-the-dark output. The back-propagation algorithm compares that output with the correct answer, supplied to the network in advance by its designer. If the answer is wrong—and it usually is, at first—the algorithm propagates an error code backward through the network, readjusting the connection strengths so that the output of the network will be more correct the next time it receives that particular input. The process is repeated until the algorithm has created a set of connection strengths that yields the smallest output errors for the input patterns the network has learned.

These two broad developments—the provision of a hidden layer of neurons and the creation of learning algorithms such as back propagation—demonstrated that many of Minsky and Papert's initial doubts about neural networks could indeed be overcome. In fact, advances in the field precipitated a sort of posthumous rapprochement between Minsky and Rosenblatt: "I now believe the book [Perceptrons] was overkill," Minsky allowed in 1981. "After being irritated with Rosenblatt for overclaiming and diverting all those people along a false path, I started to realize that for what you get out of [the perceptron]—the kind of recognition it can do—it is such a simple machine that it would be astonishing if nature did not make use of it somewhere."

Minsky chose the occasion of the second International Conference on Neural Networks, which drew 1,700 engineers, psychologists, and computer scientists to San Diego in June of 1988, to admit that "I wish I had discovered back propagation." Although Minsky applauded the advances that neural networks had made in the two decades since his book's appearance, he remained skeptical of grand claims for the devices. In the prologue to his 1988 edition of Perceptrons, for example, he and Papert stated that "We believe this realm of work to be immensely important and rich, but we expect its growth to require a degree of critical analysis that its more romantic advocates have always been reluctant to pursue." Partly to acknowledge that he and those "romantic advocates" shared a common goal, however, Minsky inscribed the updated work "In memory of Frank Rosenblatt."

IN THE IMAGE OF A CHILD

As the high attendance at the San Diego conference suggested, neural networks seem to have at last won a secure position in computer science. Keenly aware of the failed promise of earlier developments such as the perceptron, however, most neural-net researchers have adopted a deliberately modest stance. "The attitude of the new generation of scientists working on connectionist ideas is quite different from that of some AI researchers a decade or more ago," physicist

A falling broom is about to be rescued by a neural-network computer on the bottom shelf of this broom-balancing machine, built to demonstrate the ability of neural networks to respond to continuously changing circumstances. The broom's degree of tilt is sent to the computer, which issues near-instantaneous instructions to motors that reposition the supporting platform under the broom before it falls.

Heinz Pagels wrote in 1988. "People who work in this area are for the most part humbled by the enormous challenge confronting them."

Underscoring the enormity of that challenge, one observer has noted that it will be a long time before any neural net can match the mental abilities of even a three-year-old child. Indeed, that level of machine sophistication has come to represent an elusive goal for computers of all architectures, be they von Neumann or alternative. The average preschooler commands an impressive array of data-processing faculties: He or she can rapidly absorb and interpret new information, monitor the changing minutiae in a visual scene, and make educated assumptions based on a limited number of facts.

In a dramatic demonstration of how a computer might emulate the learning skills of a youngster, biophysicist Terrence Sejnowski—the man who had put the neural-net bug in John Hopfield's ear—and psychologist Charles Rosenberg in 1986 designed a network simulation that learned to pronounce written English overnight (pages 32-35). Machines capable of converting text into speech had been commercially available since 1975; in fact, Sejnowski and Rosenberg named their system NETtalk in honor of the speech-synthesis program DECtalk, which was released by the Digital Equipment Corporation in 1983.

DECtalk drew upon a pronunciation dictionary of more than 10,000 common words and nearly 500 linguistic rules for translating letters into sounds. To help the system handle the unexpected, its designer, M.I.T. programmer Dennis Klatt, furnished it with a look-up table of 6,000 words not governed by those linguistic rules, along with some simple guidelines for sounding out unfamiliar words. Together, these features gave DECtalk the ability to correctly pronounce more than 20,000 words.

Unlike its predecessor, NETtalk had no dictionary and no programmed rules for pronunciation. Instead it relied on the collective learning capacity of 309 neurons distributed among three layers: The input layer contained 203 neurons, the hidden layer 80, and the output layer 26. The neurons in this final layer activated an electronic voice synthesizer, modeled after one built by Klatt for DECtalk, that could reproduce a wide range of vocal sounds.

Like many of the experimental neural networks before it, NETtalk was simulated on a digital computer (in this case, a DEC VAX minicomputer). Words were presented to the network in the same way that alphanumeric characters are stored and manipulated in digital computers—that is, as electronic pulses representing the ones and zeros of binary code. In NETtalk's case, the initial data stream represented a "training" text of 20,012 words, and the input-layer neurons were allowed to examine this unbroken chain of information seven characters at a time. This was a crucial provision, for the pronunciation of English, like that of most other modern languages, is context dependent—that is, the sound of an individual letter often varies depending on the letters that surround it. Context dependence keeps digital-computer programs such as DECtalk from a facile mastery of spoken language: The number of rules needed to cover the pronunciation of all possible letter combinations approaches the number of such combinations themselves. This stumbling block was partly responsible for the fact that DECtalk designer Klatt had spent more than fifteen years ironing out the bugs in his creation.

NETtalk began its task with every one of the 18,629 connections among its various layers of neurons set to small, random values. Each time a seven-letter sequence was shown to the input layer, NETtalk took a stab at pronouncing the middle letter of the seven. The sequence was then advanced by one letter, and NETtalk did its best to sound out the next character that had taken up the middle position. The initial result of this "wild-guess" approach, remarked computer scientist Colin Johnson, was "a continuous, voiced wail with no intelligible characteristics." With NETtalk's every exposure to the training sample, however, its back-propagation algorithm came into play, electronically readjusting the neurons' interconnections so that the system's pronunciation gradually converged on a prespecified "ideal" pronunciation. In NETtalk's case, this ideal was a phonetic transcription of a body of text that had been read aloud by a six-year-old. Within a few hours, the system had discovered word boundaries—that is, the spaces that separate letters into words. This key pronunciation cue inaugurated a babbling, babylike phase as NETtalk began to reproduce the cadences of human speech, which in turn led to clearly recognizable utterances.

Within just twelve hours, NETtalk was reading the training text with 95 percent accuracy. Although such performance fell short of DECtalk and its 97 percent accuracy, NETtalk had demonstrated that a machine mimicking the computational style of the human brain could be taught to master complex tasks.

COMPUTERS THAT SEE AND HEAR

Neural networks may be the key to unlocking all manner of additional pattern-recognition problems. In 1983, for example, Brown University physicists Leon Cooper and Charles Elbaum founded a neural-network company called Nestor (after the Greek general known for his wisdom) whose products are designed to recognize the patterns in everything from the handwritten numbers and signatures on personal checks to the metal nuts and bolts rolling off an assembly line.

Cooper and Elbaum had first joined forces in 1975, when they formed a limited partnership to explore the commercial prospects for neural nets. Eight years later, they released Nestor's first product, a simulated neural network that could recognize characters as they were drawn by hand on a touch-sensitive pad. A more sophisticated version of this simulation, called NestorWriter, was able to recognize the 2,500 most commonly used ideograms that make up kanji, the Japanese writing system that is based on Chinese characters. Character recognizers employing neural-network technology have immense commercial appeal in Japan, where the development of conventional word processing has been thwarted by the sheer magnitude of entering kanji symbols into a computer. Japanese typists must grapple with keyboards covered by as many as 3,200 kanji characters, a number that makes it impossible to design the sort of compact keyboards that handle the twenty-six letters of the Roman alphabet. Promising relief from such awkwardness, NestorWriter would allow individuals to enter kanji characters in a word-processing computer simply by scribbling the symbols on an attached touch-sensitive pad. The network's learning algorithm would help it adapt to each user's own unique handwriting.

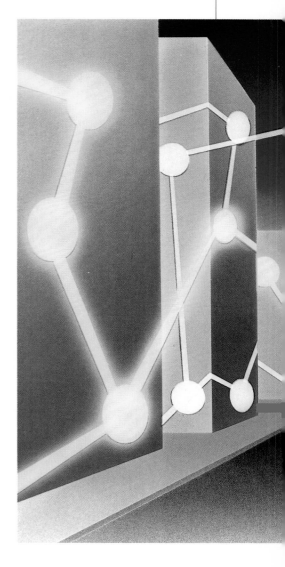

Neural networks intended to comprehend the spoken rather than written word also show great promise. Such machines, when they are finally perfected, might revolutionize the computer's place in industry, business, and the home: Factory workers could instruct robots to fetch parts from the warehouse, office workers could dictate letters and memos directly into their word processors, and family members could order personal computers to turn lights on and off, adjust the thermostat, or call up financial records.

Although several dozen software programs have been written to give elementary powers of speech comprehension to digital machines, most such programs are speaker-dependent; that is, they recognize the speech of the human masters who devised the system, but no one else's. Even those programs that are speaker-independent can understand only a limited vocabulary of about forty words. According to one estimate, developing a wholly speaker-independent digital system that could recognize 20,000 words would require computing power equal to that of 100 supercomputers combined.

But neural networks are another story. In 1988, electrical engineer Teuvo Kohonen, an influential neural-net theorist at Finland's Helsinki University of Technology, devised a network that acted as a "phonetic typewriter," taking dictation from spoken words. Kohonen's work had formed the basis for a number of associative-memory networks developed during the 1970s. Although his phonetic typewriter was not entirely speaker-independent, a prototype managed to recognize 92 to 97 percent of the everyday speech uttered by half a dozen speakers. For an unfamiliar voice to be enrolled in the network, Kohonen reported, the new speaker had only to dictate about a hundred words to the device; within ten minutes the system could recognize the bulk of his or her speech.

Like NestorWriter, Kohonen's creation may find an important market in Japan. Finnish and Japanese share some remarkably similar characteristics: The grammar in both is implemented by vocal inflections, for example, and root words in each language typically spawn dozens of different forms. Some Japanese firms such as Asahi Chemical, Fujitsu, NEC, and Toshiba have therefore expressed interest in adapting the phonetic typewriter for their own use. Meanwhile, a government-sponsored research institute in Osaka known as ATR (for Advanced Telecommunications Research) has begun a fifteen-year, $5 billion investigation of simultaneous machine translation—the computerized conversion of one spoken language to another in real time—including the role that neural networks might play in such an application.

NEURAL NETS MADE REAL

Computer scientists have long chafed at the inefficiency of simulating neural networks on standard machines. As neural nets attracted more attention during the 1980s, therefore, efforts to manufacture neural chips got under way.

Advances in this domain have occurred at a much swifter rate than the gradual pace of progress that typified neural-net research in academe during the 1970s. By the end of the 1980s, more than two dozen private companies—including such high-tech colossi as Bell Labs, IBM, Intel, Motorola, Texas Instruments, and TRW—had undertaken the design of chips that promise to form the foundation of working neurocomputers.

Three early architects of neural chips were physicists Hans Peter Graf, Richard Howard, and Lawrence Jackel of AT&T Bell Labs. The trio had been simulating large neural networks on digital computers since 1984—ample time to convince them that such exercises were "painfully slow." Only with customized hardware, the three men believed, "can we hope to realize neural-network models with speeds fast enough for applications." In 1986, the researchers created a neural-net chip, containing 54 neurons and 2,916 programmable interconnections, that could recognize handwritten numbers from zero to nine.

A network using the chip, Jackel explained, "looks for the distinguishing features of the number: A figure 3 is three horizontal lines, three stops, and two vertical lines." Graf noted that the chip could recognize handwritten digits —even those that were sloppily written—with an average accuracy of more than 94 percent. Such a system would be of immense value to, say, the United States Postal Service, which could use it to accelerate its automatic reading of envelopes addressed by hand.

Another neural-chip pioneer of the 1980s was Robert Hecht-Nielsen, who had been alerted to the networks' potential in 1968 by the writings of Boston University's Stephen Grossberg. Like the three-man team at AT&T, Hecht-Nielsen was frustrated by the plodding pace of neural-net programs running on digital machines. "It took the patience of a Gregor Mendel to do computer simulations of neural networks," he says.

After starting up a neural-network program at Motorola in 1979, Hecht-Nielsen went to work in 1983 for a conglomerate called TRW at the company's Rancho Carmel Artificial Intelligence Center near San Diego. There he helped build neurocomputers of ever-increasing sophistication. TRW's Mark III, released in 1985, featured 65,000 simulated neurons. The firm's Mark IV neurocomputer, shipped quietly to the Defense Advanced Research Projects Agency for top-secret testing under "real-world" conditions in 1986, boasted 250,000 neurons and 5.5 million interconnections.

For more than a decade, Hecht-Nielsen had studied the capabilities of specialized neural-network chips, and he was so taken with their promise that in the fall of 1986 he left TRW to found his own firm, Hecht-Nielsen Neurocomputers (HNC). In 1988, HNC won a $50,000 study grant from DARPA to investigate the development of a neural chip that could process visual images—a task that demands unusually intensive computations.

To help him design the chip, designated the 200X, Hecht-Nielsen recruited a number of leading lights in the neural-net arena. Stephen Grossberg and a fellow professor at Boston University, computer scientist Ennio Mingolla, contributed a "boundary-contour system" that would allow the chip to distinguish the edges of an object. This had always been a daunting obstacle to machine vision because real-life images are usually much more complex than they appear to the lens of a camera: Objects overlap, or they seem to be different sizes depending on their distance from the camera, or they bear markings that resemble edges but are not. Papers written by scientists Christof Koch of Caltech and Tomaso Poggio of M.I.T., meanwhile, suggested means for endowing the 200X with the capacity to detect motion.

Incorporating a number of 200X chips in a neural network, DARPA hopes, may some day yield a computer system able to detect and track enemy targets. The completed chip might even find commercial use in such high-speed machine-vision systems as those dedicated to inspecting the surface texture of newly minted VLSI (Very Large-Scale Integration) silicon wafers. In the event, a neural chip would wind up passing judgment on its silicon antecedents.

Carver Mead, who pioneered VLSI silicon-chip design in 1977, has since focused his energies on designing a neural chip that, like those under development at AT&T and HNC, may help neural networks achieve the goal of machine vision. Mead, a solid-state physicist at the California Institute of Technology, built the first commercially successful gallium-arsenide transistor in 1965. He and a Xerox Corporation computer scientist named Lynn Conway then went on to write a book, *Introduction to VLSI Systems*, that described how to expand the use of computers in designing silicon chips for other computers and paved the way for the mass production of such chips.

In 1984, inspired by some late-night talks he had had with a group of Caltech neurobiologists, Mead began crafting a chip—in effect, a tiny silicon retina—that uses neural-network principles to outperform digital supercomputers at tracking an object across its visual field. Containing 100,000 transistors, Mead's chip is superior to conventional cameras as well as computers; it can adjust its processing of optical signals to account for the presence of both light and shade in the same viewing area.

During the two years required to perfect the retinal chip, Mead grew increasingly rapt with the powers of the human sensory system to process information. His fascination led him to create an artificial cochlea, or synthetic ear, in 1985. Drawing on neural-net techniques similar to those in the retinal chip, the artificial cochlea can perform the initial stages of auditory information processing. In humans, these preprocessing steps are crucial, because they convert sounds reaching the ear into a form that can be sent to the brain for more sophisticated processing.

The images below trace the process used by a TRW Mark IV neuro-computer to identify aircraft from overhead infrared (IR) photos. First, an IR picture, revealing heat distribution within the target, is digitized and color coded; red signifies the hottest areas, concentrated around the engines (1). Next, the computer mathematically transforms the data (2) into a version (3) that can be compared to kindred views stored in a database (4). The Mark IV can choose correctly from the database 95 percent of the time (5), unconfused by differences in aircraft orientation or by such subtleties as wing angle in aircraft having variable-sweep wings.

Convinced that design breakthroughs such as these were marketable, Mead and his longtime colleague Federico Faggin—who had aided Ted Hoff in designing Intel's first microprocessor circuits—helped found a company called Synaptics (after the synapses, or interconnections, of neural networks). Synaptics began designing neural chips for a wide range of pattern-recognition tasks, primarily those involving the identification of sound waves from sources as diverse as the human larynx and a patrolling submarine.

NEURAL NETS AT WAR

DARPA's funding of the 200X neural chip was but one example of the military's appetite for alternative computers of every description. Neural nets may indeed lend themselves to all sorts of modern military applications, psychologist James Anderson has pointed out, because current and future generations of "smart" weapons are being imbued with unmistakably animal-like traits: "Animals, warships, and aircraft all have to evade pursuers, work with noisy data, head for targets, and make guesses. They must also be fast, general-purpose, damage-resistant, and 'pretty good' in their behavior, but none of them has the time to wait around to become entirely error-free."

In a demonstration of a neural net meeting some of those high expectations, University of Pennsylvania radar-and-optics expert Nabil Farhat created a neural network in 1985 that could transform the radar signals reflected from an aircraft into a label or a realistic image of the plane itself, complete with wings and engines. When prompted with only about 20 percent of the radar profile of an airplane, Farhat's network retrieved from its memory a complete matching image of the craft. A fighter plane or bomber equipped with such a network would enjoy a tactical edge in aerial combat because it could identify enemy

3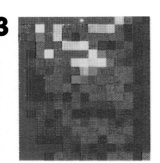

4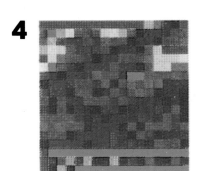

5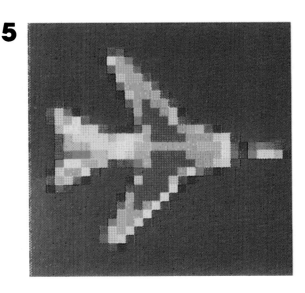

aircraft on the basis of partial radar returns. Such incomplete radar data is typical of that produced by an airplane's search-and-location radar when it first picks up a distant target.

The military is especially eager to adapt neural networks for battlefield use because the machines exhibit a trait that computer scientists call graceful degradation: With the storage and processing of information in a neural net distributed among its many neurons, the network can often continue functioning even when part of it has been damaged. "Our customers like the idea that a neural net might be able to take a few bullets and keep on running," says Robert Hecht-Nielsen of his work on neurocomputers for DARPA. Indeed, graceful degradation—and, by extension, any neural network that displays it—would be a boon for any number of electronic instruments that must function in remote locales: NASA probes navigating the immensity of space, underground sensors detecting the onset of earthquakes, or eavesdropping devices collecting signals intelligence from far-off mountains or near-earth orbits.

... AND MILES TO GO BEFORE THEY THINK

For all the scientific and commercial interest they have sparked in recent years, neural networks have yet to emerge fully from their chrysalis. If research and development are to evolve from their current embryonic stage, psychologists and neurobiologists must map out the intricate paths by which information is processed in the brain, and engineers and computer scientists must convert the resulting knowledge diagrams into neural chips and networks.

It may therefore be a long time before anyone builds a device that rivals the remarkable machinery at work inside the human mind, or even an insect mind. On the distant day when such an alternative computer is unveiled, it will likely embody both the intuitive pattern-matching abilities of neural networks and the precise serial processing of conventional machines. The two approaches to computation would thus wind up complementing—rather than competing with —each other. Such a synthesis would bear out the newer prognostications of Marvin Minsky and Seymour Papert. Twenty years after their critique of the original neural network, the perceptron, the two men conceded that AI and neural nets are both attempting to shed light on a computing mechanism that science remains far from comprehending. "Maybe," wrote Minsky and Papert in their 1988 epilogue to *Perceptrons,* "since the brain is a hierarchy of systems, the best machine will be too."

A Way to Compute with Light

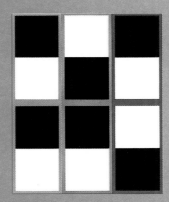

The power of a computer is traditionally measured in terms of how quickly it can perform calculations. Conventional serial computers have always been limited by having to churn through operations one step at a time. Parallel architectures, in which many processors work on data simultaneously, provide one way around the sequential slowdown, but even the speediest of these machines can be delayed by having to wait for electrical signals to travel through mazes of circuitry. In the perpetual quest for greater speed, computer designers are now turning to a whole new computing medium: light.

Light not only is the fastest thing in the universe but also lends itself to parallelism in ways unattainable with electrons. Unlike electrical signals, light rays do not interfere with one another if their paths cross. Thus, many different encoded beams of light can easily travel together—through optical fibers or even free space—and be processed simultaneously. The parallel electronic computer, on the other hand, must go to great lengths to ensure that individual data channels are sufficiently isolated from one another to avoid interference and the corrupting influence of noise from nearby wiring.

Researchers have proposed a number of different optical computer designs. Some of these prospective machines would use visible light, others infrared. The components themselves could range from the familiar to the far-out. In the theoretical example on the following pages, simple lenses would take care of much of the routing work, but complex devices would also be needed for some of the more technically sophisticated processes involved.

An Interplay of Functional Elements

The most familiar aspect of any proposed optical computer design is the approach to processing illustrated below—an organizational scheme inherited from electronic digital computers. But in the functional areas represented by the blocks, the optical computer's implementation would be radically different. Where an electronic computer has transistors and circuitry for, say, storing data in memory or carrying out logic operations, an optical computer would use an array of light-manipulating devices ranging from relatively simple lenses and mirrors to sophisticated, exotic-sounding components such as spatial light modulators and Fourier transform masks.

Because input and output would presumably pass through an electrical stage on their way between the optical computer and the outside world, some components would handle conversions from one medium to the other. This encoding and decoding of light would permit links with all types of tradi-

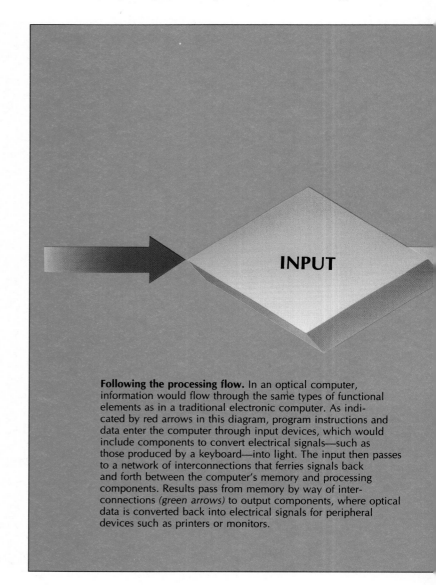

INPUT

Following the processing flow. In an optical computer, information would flow through the same types of functional elements as in a traditional electronic computer. As indicated by red arrows in this diagram, program instructions and data enter the computer through input devices, which would include components to convert electrical signals—such as those produced by a keyboard—into light. The input then passes to a network of interconnections that ferries signals back and forth between the computer's memory and processing components. Results pass from memory by way of interconnections (green arrows) to output components, where optical data is converted back into electrical signals for peripheral devices such as printers or monitors.

tional electronic peripheral devices, such as keyboards, printers, disk drives, and even other computers. But the optical computer's overall speed would inevitably be limited by the relatively slow electronic components with which it interacts.

The main advantages of optics lie in the transportation of data within the computer and the actual processing of that data through the execution of logic operations. The interconnections forming an optical computer's communications network would pay handsome speed dividends by carrying light signals either through optical fibers that bend around curves or through free space in straight lines, in either case outstripping the swiftest of conventional electrical circuits. And, as explained on the next two pages, a digital optical computer could perform logic in ways designed to exploit opportunities for parallel processing, thereby providing the possibility of exponential improvements in execution time.

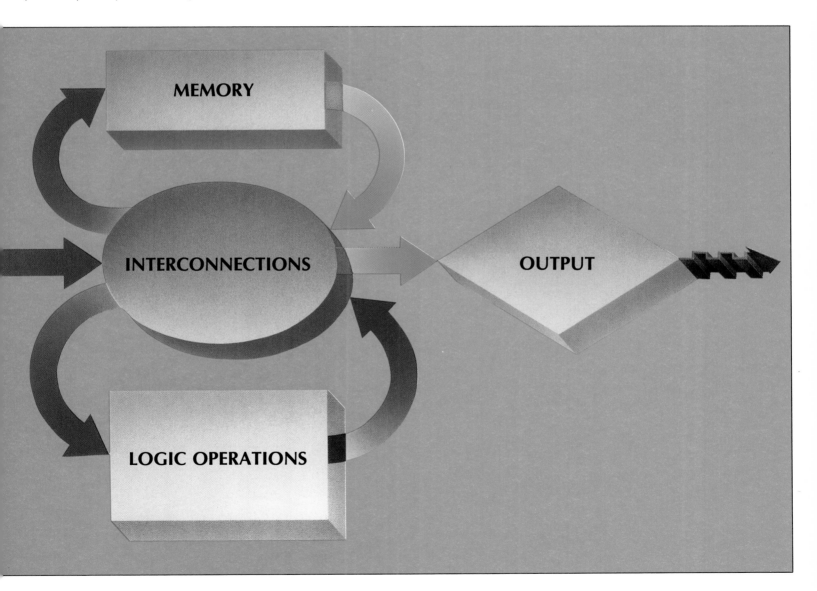

A Way to Compute with Light

Decimal	Binary	Binary
0	0	
1	1	
2	10	
3	11	
4	100	
5	101	
6	110	
7	111	
8	1000	
9	1001	
10	1010	

A table of equivalents. The decimal numbers zero to ten are shown above in binary form both as sequences of zeros and ones and as optical patterns of bright and dark squares, with each binary digit represented by a vertical pair of squares; zeros are dark on top, ones bright. In both binary codes, each place column to the left represents the next highest power of two.

When adding two binary digits, an optical computer must be able to recognize light patterns for the four possible combinations of a zero and a one, as shown at right in the left-hand column. Following the rules illustrated here, the computer substitutes a new pattern that represents the result of the operation *(right column)*. The pattern in the lower right of each answer represents the sum, while that in the upper left is a carry to the next place column.

Rules for Optical Logic

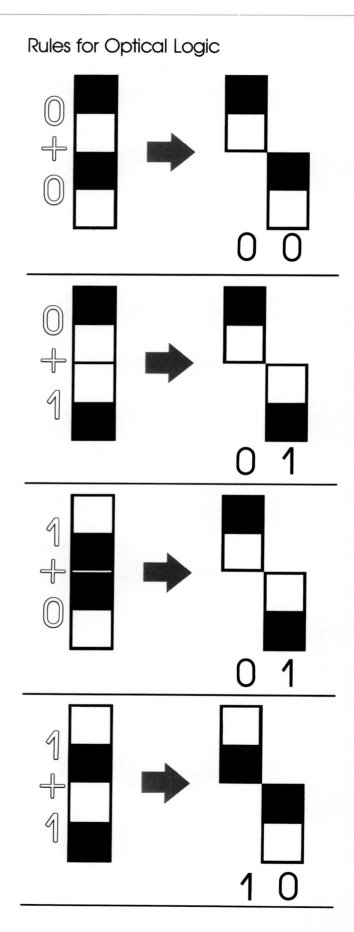

A Binary Code for Optical Adding

At the heart of all digital processing lies a simple concept: the encoding of data in binary form, as groups of zeros and ones. To perform arithmetic, for example, a digital computer has to manipulate only two different digits rather than the ten of decimal notation. Electronic computers represent these two binary digits, or bits, with electrical signals that either pulse on and off or switch between a high and a low voltage. Optical computers would use similar techniques with light, noting its absence or presence or distinguishing between two different brightness levels.

The optical code illustrated here symbolizes each bit with a pattern of two vertically stacked squares, one bright and one dark; a bright square on top denotes a one. This approach, though seemingly less efficient than assigning one square per bit, simplifies identification because the computer need only determine which of the two squares is brighter, without having to analyze their specific intensity values.

Hand in hand with any code are the rules for manipulat-

ing that code to perform logic operations. The code in this example is suited to a type of logic known as symbolic substitution, in which the optical system first recognizes input patterns symbolizing zeros and ones, then substitutes the appropriate output patterns. Because substitutions can be made simultaneously wherever a particular input pattern occurs, this method is key to the optical computer's ability to process in parallel; a conventional electronic computer would have to send each calculation in turn through a single processor.

Substitution patterns differ depending on the specific type of calculation being performed. For addition *(left)*, the output patterns are designed to effect carrying; the diagonal offset is equivalent to writing a carry digit at the top of an addition column. The following pages trace the solution of the simple addition problem outlined below through the various optical components that are needed for each step of the computing process.

Combining Multiple Sums and Carries

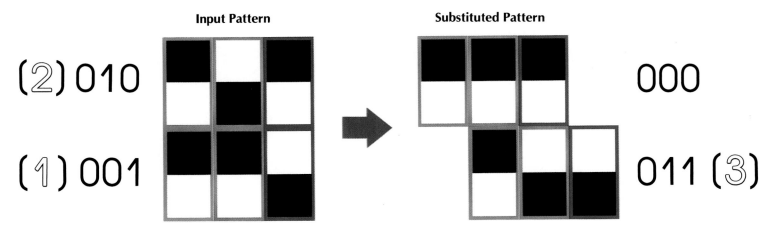

Input Pattern   **Substituted Pattern**

(2) 010
(1) 001

000
011 (3)

The same rules of pattern substitution illustrated at left apply for adding multiple-digit binary numbers, such as the two three-digit numbers shown above (a column of zeros is always added to the left to cover the possibility of the answer including a carry from the previous place column). Each four-square column is replaced with

the appropriate sum-and-carry pattern so that the first column's carry stacks over the next column's sum, and so on *(above)*. The answer—011, or 3—appears in the lower, sum half of the new pattern; had there been any ones in the upper, carry half, further substitutions would have been performed until all the carries were zeros.

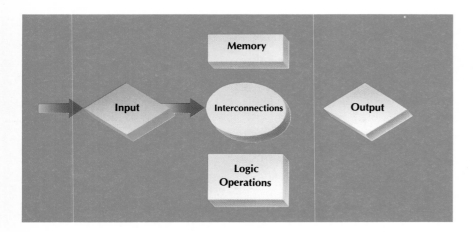

Generating a Pattern with Polarized Light

A magnetic array. Each cell in the array below is composed of a compound of the metals yttrium and iron, which has been magnetized in one of two directions *(purple arrows)* by electrical signals from an input device such as a keyboard. Every vertical pair of cells represents a separate zero or one of binary input.

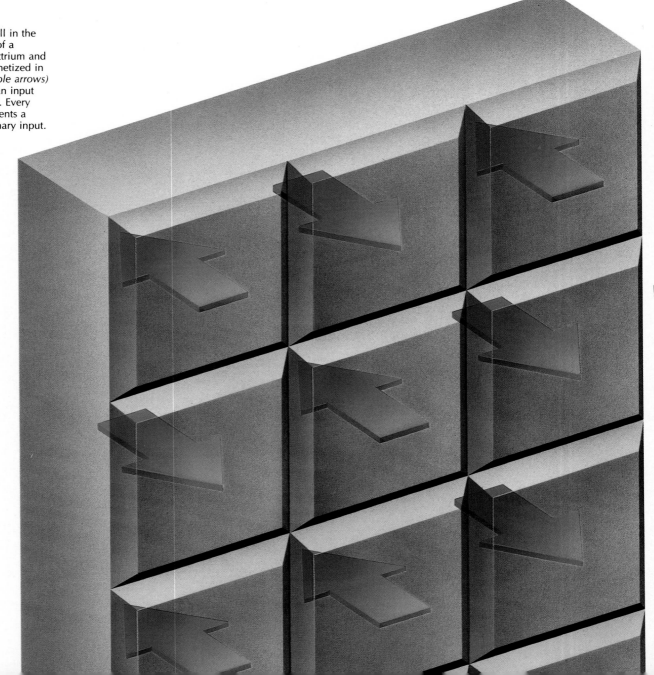

The first stage in optical processing is, of course, the input of data *(far left)*, which requires transforming electrical input signals into an optical form. The devices that accomplish this critical task are known as spatial light modulators because they change, or modulate, the cross-sectional pattern of a beam of light. While some spatial light modulators affect the way light reflects off them *(pages 82-83)*, the one diagrammed here alters light transmitted through it, by means of a combination of electromagnetic and optical effects.

The technique relies on a special property of laser light, which would be used in an optical computer. Ordinary light contains a mixture of waves vibrating in different directions, but the waves of laser light vibrate, or are polarized, in only one direction, in this case vertically. By altering the polarization of this light in two different directions, the spatial light modulator creates an optical binary code.

The modulator below is a sandwich of two types of components, shown for clarity as separate elements. The first consists of a layer of magnetic material divided into an array of cells, each of which receives a separate electrical signal that affects its magnetic polarity; this magnetic polarity in turn affects how light passing through it will be polarized. The second component is a polarizing filter designed to transmit only those light waves polarized in one particular direction. The result is an optical pattern of bright and dark squares equivalent to the original pattern of binary electrical signals.

Only twelve cells are shown in this simplified example, corresponding to the twelve bright and dark squares necessary for the addition problem introduced on page 73. Actual arrays could contain more than 100 cells on a side, thereby providing ample opportunities for parallel execution during symbolic substitution.

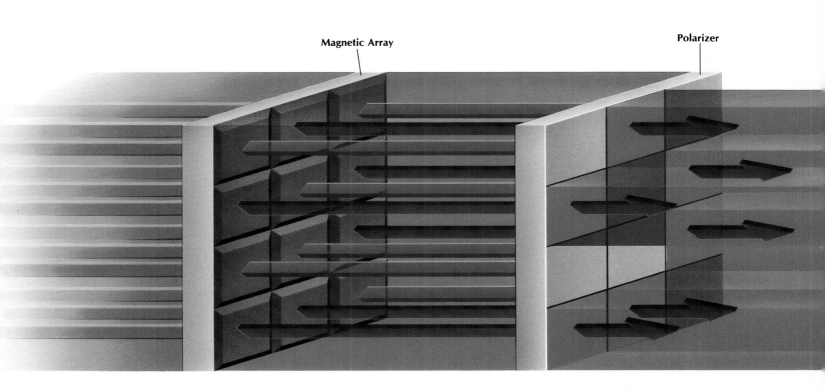

Magnetic Array

Polarizer

Altering light's polarity. Depending on its direction of magnetization, each cell in the array changes the polarization angle of vertically polarized light from a laser *(red ribbons)*. Cells magnetized toward the input beam rotate the polarity forty-five degrees clockwise, while those magnetized in the opposite direction turn polarization forty-five degrees counterclockwise.

Creating a bright-dark pattern. The polarization pattern is changed to an array of bright and dark zones as it passes through a polarizer. Light is transmitted if its polarization was rotated counterclockwise, but blocked if its polarization shifted in the opposite direction. The array of twelve cells forms the complete code of zeros and ones for adding 2 + 1.

A Way to Compute with Light

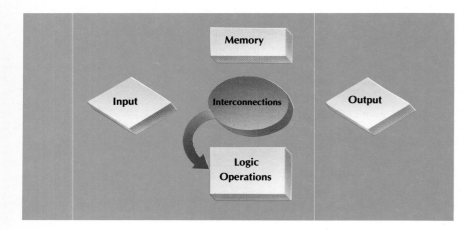

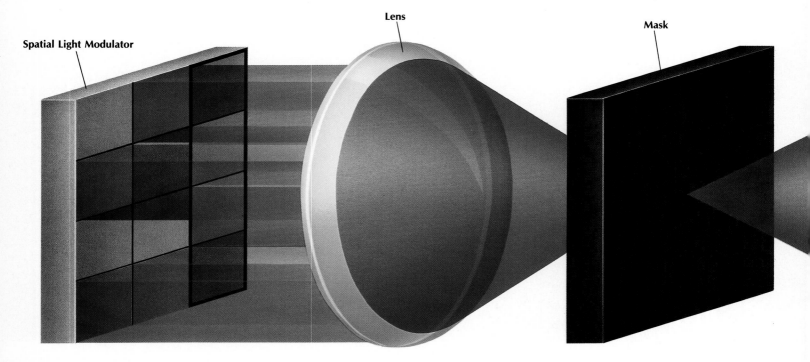

Spatial Light Modulator

Lens

Mask

The input pattern produced by the spatial light modulator consists of three columns of four squares apiece, each representing a place column in the addition problem. The right-hand column *(outlined in bold)* contains the bright and dark squares representing 0 + 1.

A convex lens captures the entire input pattern and focuses it to a point, projecting it onto a mask lying in the lens's focal plane.

The mask is a specially designed component that recognizes and transmits selected patterns; here, it identifies and forwards only that part of the focused image representing 0 + 1. Later, the mask will be reconfigured for each of the three other possible patterns of zeros and ones.

Transmitting and Recognizing the Code

Once the beam of laser light has been properly encoded by a spatial light modulator, it must be transported to those parts of the computer where symbolic substitution takes place. It is in the means of transmitting this data that optical computers can far outshine their electronic counterparts; using a system of lenses and other components, the interconnections of an optical computer transform and then retransform the coded patterns so that many data elements can be forwarded all at once, instead of in sequence.

The secret lies in the natural ability of lenses to perform a complex mathematical function known as the Fourier transform. In essence, Fourier transforms render complex phenomena into a form in which their simpler constituent elements can be more easily identified. In the scheme shown here, a lens focuses an input beam consisting of several different patterns. Identical patterns will overlap in the lens's focal plane. Thus, multiple occurrences of the same pattern can be identified simultaneously.

The components on these two pages handle the initial recognition phase of symbolic substitution and are shown identifying the input pattern representing 0 + 1; the substitution of the new pattern that symbolizes the sum of these digits is demonstrated on the next two pages. For clarity, the selected pattern occurs only once on this small array, but the optics would recognize it concurrently no matter how many times it appeared and wherever it was.

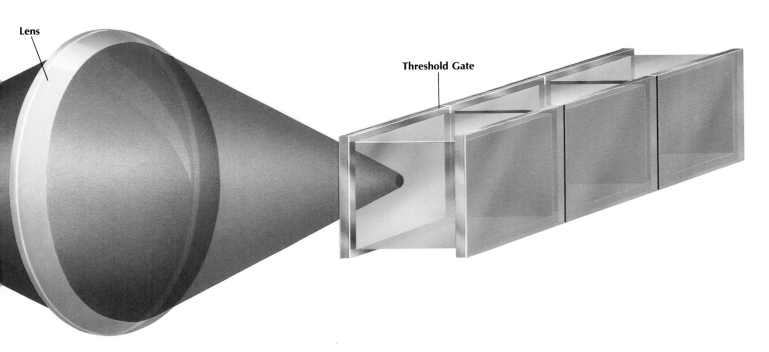

Lens

Threshold Gate

Light transmitted by the mask passes to a second convex lens. The lens again focuses the light to a point, this time projecting it onto a threshold gate—explained on pages 78 and 79.

The threshold gate consists of three blocks, corresponding to the three columns in the original input pattern. Passing light through two lenses reverses images from right to left; thus, the bright spot in the left-hand block represents the 0 + 1 pattern from the right-hand column of the input array.

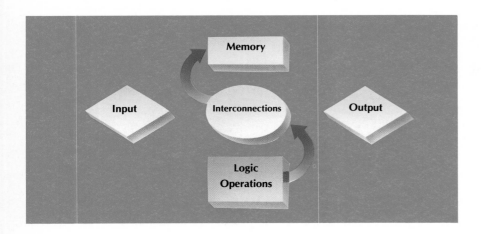

Transforming a Point Back into a Pattern

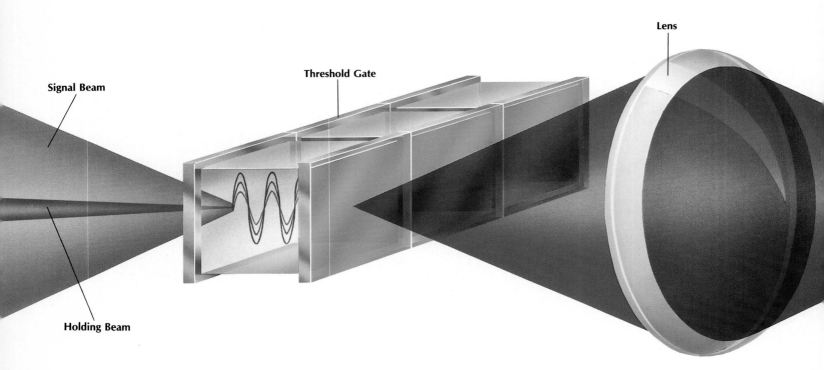

Signal Beam

Holding Beam

Threshold Gate

Lens

At the threshold gate, the weakened signal beam combines with a holding beam from a separate laser. Resounding back and forth in phase within the threshold gate *(wavy lines)*, light waves from the two beams reinforce each other; when the light reaches a certain intensity, the threshold gate passes it on.

The first lens of the substitution phase collects light from the threshold gate and focuses it onto the substitution mask *(right)*. The light retains the information that came from the left-hand block of the threshold gate.

The second stage of the optical computer's logic operations —the substituting of new patterns—involves a similar set of lenses for transporting data and masks for processing it. The masks employed in the recognition phase, however, are only responsible for identifying the location of patterns from the input array; substitution masks, on the other hand, perform processing chores more closely akin to the work of an electronic computer's logic gates, transforming input signals into the appropriate output patterns.

The two stages are connected by a device called a threshold gate *(far left)*, which transmits light only if it exceeds a certain brightness. Much like an electronic repeater or amplifier, this component helps boost signal beams, which tend to weaken as they make their way through other components. It also keeps stray light from triggering an incorrect substitution.

Coordination of processing activities is as crucial in optical as in electronic computing. Spots of light transmitted by the threshold gate only indicate where a particular pattern is located, not which one it is; thus the substitution and recognition masks must be configured for the same type of pattern at the same time. Because in this simple two-bit addition problem there are four possible combinations of zeros and ones *(pages 72-73)*, the process of recognition and substitution would be repeated four times, with the two masks simultaneously reconfigured for a different pattern each time.

As in the recognition phase, the lenses enable many identical patterns to be processed in parallel. Had the 0 + 1 pattern occurred in all three place columns of the input array, each block of the threshold gate would have transmitted a bright spot and the first lens would have forwarded all three at once, focusing them to a single point. Having been transformed by the substitution mask, the focused spot would have then been reconverted by the second lens into three identical replacement patterns, ready to be forwarded to memory.

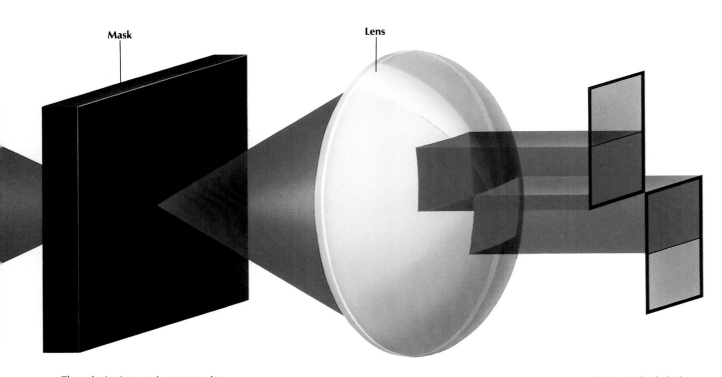

Mask

Lens

The substitution mask converts the point of light into the appropriate substitution pattern representing the sum of 0 + 1. A second lens *(right)* completes the transformation process, focusing light from the mask into the recognizable diagonal pattern *(far right)*.

Because the light has passed through two lenses and been reversed a second time, the substituted pattern appears properly oriented and will correspond to the position of the original input pattern.

A Way to Compute with Light

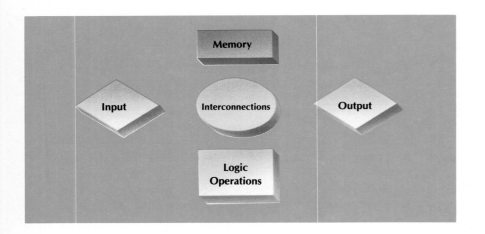

A sandwich of components. A combination of electrical and optical components forms a memory array for the optical computer *(right)*. Voltage applied to transparent electrodes at either end of the sandwich sets up an electric field. A photoconductor layer, made of a material that conducts electricity only where it is struck by light, isolates the liquid-crystal layer from the field except at points where data is actually stored.

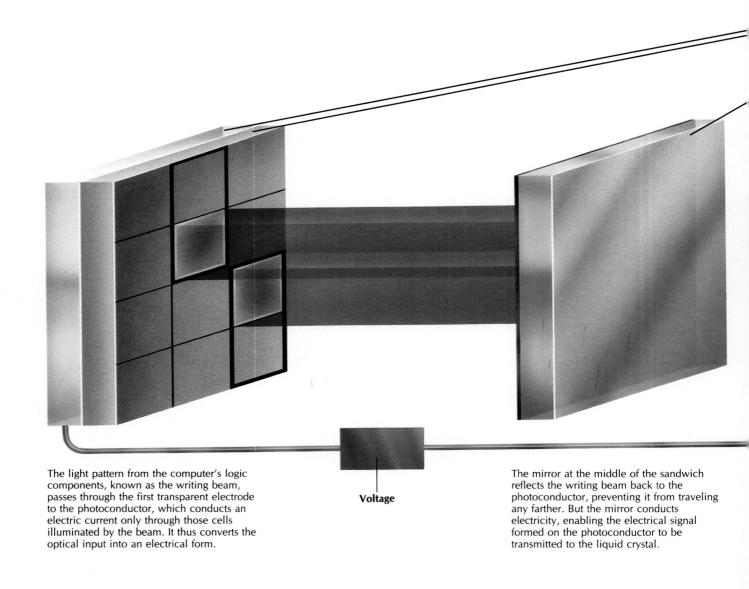

The light pattern from the computer's logic components, known as the writing beam, passes through the first transparent electrode to the photoconductor, which conducts an electric current only through those cells illuminated by the beam. It thus converts the optical input into an electrical form.

Voltage

The mirror at the middle of the sandwich reflects the writing beam back to the photoconductor, preventing it from traveling any farther. But the mirror conducts electricity, enabling the electrical signal formed on the photoconductor to be transmitted to the liquid crystal.

Photoconductor
Electrode
Mirror
Liquid Crystal
Electrode

An Optical Memory for Storing Patterns

One function of computer memory is the temporary storage of results from incomplete calculations. Known as random-access memory, this type of memory serves as a kind of scratch pad, like numbers written below the dividend in long division, holding information needed for the final result. In electronic computers, specially designed integrated circuits store individual units of data by the thousands in tiny devices called capacitors; typically, a charged capacitor represents a one, a discharged capacitor a zero.

An optical computer performing symbolic substitution also needs a scratch-pad memory because it processes input in stages—one stage for each optical pattern it recognizes. An initial round of substitutions, such as for the 0 + 1 pattern in this example, must be remembered until all the other substitutions have taken place and a final result can be compiled. One method for storing this optical data makes use of a different kind of spatial light modulator than that designed for the initial input of data *(pages 74-75)*; instead of converting electrical signals into patterns of light, the memory version converts the light patterns into electrical charges that can be retained while the computer runs through other processing cycles. When it comes time to read the contents of memory *(pages 82-83)*, the electrical signals are transformed back into light for the computer's optical circuitry.

The crucial element in the memory modulator is a layer of liquid crystal, the material that allows figures to be displayed continuously on a digital watch. Because its optical properties can be influenced by electrical charges, the liquid crystal makes the conversion back into light possible.

The two bright spots of the writing beam are stored in the liquid crystal as areas of increased voltage. The liquid crystal thus replicates the substitution pattern *(outlined in bold)* and will retain it while other patterns are processed.

A Way to Compute with Light

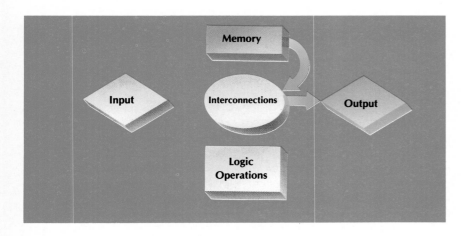

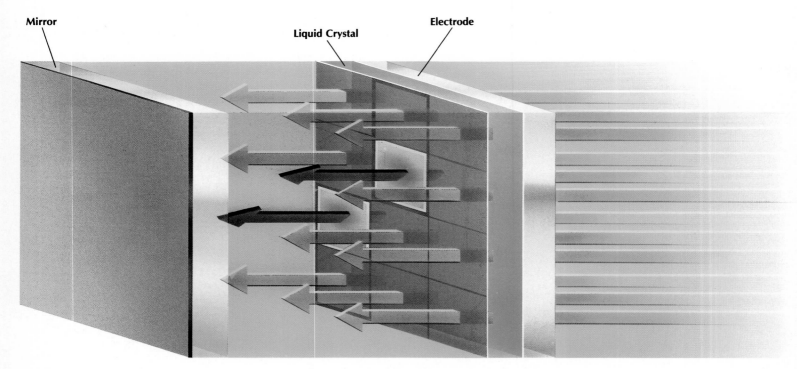

A reading beam of vertically polarized laser light *(green arrows)* enters the memory array from the right, passing first through the transparent electrode and then the liquid crystal. Liquid-crystal cells that were affected by an electric charge rotate the light's polarization by forty-five degrees *(dark green);* other cells leave the polarization unchanged.

A New Beam of Light for Reading Memory

The optical computer interacts with its memory components in a two-stage process. As explained on pages 80 and 81, optical data is written into memory in the form of electrically altered areas in a layer of liquid crystal. This liquid crystal is a spatial light modulator and acts on a new beam of laser light, known as the reading beam *(here represented as green)*.

Like the spatial light modulator used for converting electrical input signals, the modulator for memory works by rotating the direction in which light is polarized. At the input stage, the rotation occurs in two opposite directions, forty-five degrees each way; the result is a discrepancy of ninety degrees in polarization, which the polarizer element needs to distinguish one set of signals from the other and create a pattern of bright and dark zones. In memory, the approach is slightly different: Since only bright areas are stored, the liquid crystal that causes the polarization change must do so twice. As demonstrated below, a simple mirror that sends the reading beam back through the liquid crystal a second time accomplishes the required shift of ninety degrees and allows the stored pattern to be discerned.

Stored data transformed back into light requires further translation before it can finally leave the computer as output. Any of a number of different light-detecting devices can take care of this task, converting the light's intensity into the streams of electrical signals that drive conventional output devices such as printers or monitors.

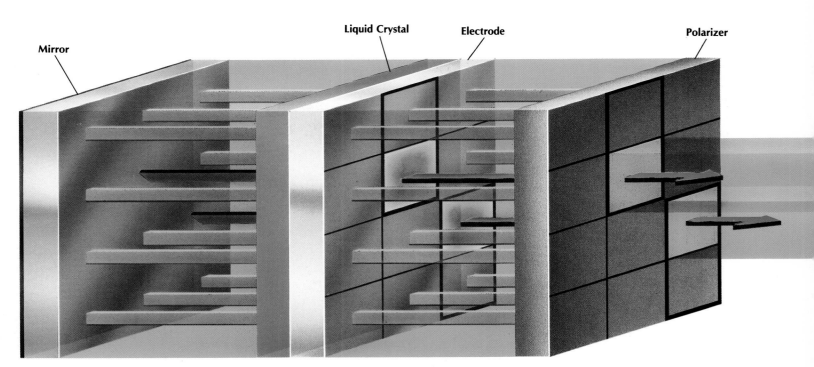

Mirror   **Liquid Crystal**   **Electrode**   **Polarizer**

The mirror that reflected the writing beam off its left surface reflects the rays of the reading beam off its right surface without affecting their direction of polarization.

Light reflected from the mirror passes a second time through the liquid crystal. The electrically altered cells rotate the light's polarization another forty-five degrees *(dark green arrows)*. Light emerging from the liquid crystal thus is polarized either vertically or horizontally.

A polarizer converts the polarization pattern into differences in intensity by transmitting only horizontally polarized light; vertically polarized rays are blocked. Thus the data is once again represented in the optical code of bright and dark zones.

Of Photons, Atoms, and Molecules

A picosecond lasts one-trillionth of one-sixtieth of one minute. Although almost unimaginably small, this sliver of time is far from inconsequential in the world of computing. For example, supercomputer designers anticipate that the fastest machines on their drawing boards will need more than four hundred picoseconds to execute a binary operation. The trip from memory to the central processing unit might take as long as a thousand picoseconds. To switch each of the transistors in such a computer from on to off or vice versa consumes six or seven picoseconds.

But if light instead of electricity were traveling through the circuitry, data coming from memory would reach the CPU in about 300 picoseconds. And the time required to cycle optical computing elements from one state to another might take as little as 1/1,000 the time required by a transistor. In 1987, researchers at AT&T Bell Laboratories created a flash of laser light that lasted 6/1,000 of a picosecond.

On speed of data transmission alone, an optical digital computer might be expected to function at least ten times faster than the electronic equivalent. Taking into account the effects of greater switching speed, it is easy to imagine an optical computer that performs a hundred times faster than the electronic version. And that could be just the beginning. Optics encourages abandonment of the venerable, step-at-a-time von Neumann way of computing. The ultimate speed in optical computing, most experts agree, lies in the direction of processing many instructions in parallel. Because light beams do not influence each other as electric currents do when they cross paths or travel close to one another, optical parallel processors promise to be much easier to build compactly than electronic ones.

But light is not the only route to computers far more powerful than those possible with today's technology. Some researchers think of tomorrow's computers in almost organic terms, envisioning machines built of molecules not too different from those that constitute life on this planet. Organic chemists skilled in the art of constructing molecules for virtually any biological purpose—from attacking cancer cells to repairing ulcers—have already combined hydrogen, carbon, nitrogen, and oxygen atoms in molecules that behave like diodes, which permit current to flow in one direction but not the other. Not far in the future, practitioners of this art expect to create memory cells and logic gates of molecules that, in essence, would assemble themselves into tiny, ultrafast computers. Judging by what is already known, these devices would work electronically and could be either digital or analog machines.

Yet they may be only a technological way station. From building computers molecule by molecule, it is a short step in the scientific imagination to assembling them atom by atom. Such is the vision of Eric Drexler, a former M.I.T. research engineer who now teaches at Stanford University. He and a growing contingent of scientists see on the far horizon a technological world where dimensions are measured in nanometers (billionths of meters) and where nanocomputers guide nanomachines so small that—among other roles—hundreds of them might work unobtrusively inside the nucleus of a cell to guard human health.

THE NEAREST OF THE DISTANT

Of the various technological frontiers of computer design, optics is the best reconnoitered by far. For more than a decade, light has been used to carry data between computers and to store information for later retrieval. Both of these applications depend on the room-temperature laser diode, a small, inexpensive source of low-power laser light. Invented in 1971 at AT&T Bell Laboratories, this device was the first laser diode to operate without the need for a cooling bath of liquid nitrogen. A laser beam differs significantly from the rays of a light bulb in that its waves are coherent. That is, they emanate from the laser perfectly synchronized, traveling crest to crest and trough to trough. This feature allows a laser beam to carry information in much the same way radio waves do. Indeed, light waves are in many respects nothing more than radio waves of higher frequency.

Both can travel from source to destination through a tube called a waveguide; by internal reflection, the waves careen from side to side along the tube, even bending around corners with little loss of energy. For radio waves, the tube takes the form of a hollow pipe several inches in diameter, but for light, the waveguide is a filament of glass. Optical fibers, as they are called, have been rapidly replacing copper wires in telephone networks because of light's phenomenal information-carrying capacity. An axiom of communications, whether between telephones across town or between microchips on opposite sides of a circuit board, is that the higher the frequency of a communications medium—that is, the greater its so-called bandwidth—the more data it can handle. In a telephone network, where capacity is measured by the number of telephone conversations that can be carried simultaneously over a single path, one optical fiber can convey hundreds of thousands of such dialogues. A copper wire can carry no more than a few hundred.

The capacity and speed of fiberoptic communications have encouraged the use of light as the messenger in computer networks, from huge webs such as the Defense Department's ARPANET, which links defense-project researchers across the country, to local networks tying together a cluster of desktop computers. Fiberoptic cables are also used within computers; for example, they link the circuit boards of powerful switching computers used to make telephone connections. Even the conductive pins that connect a microprocessor in a computer with other chips inside the machine could become glass instead of metal. Metal pins, like copper wire, have a comparatively narrow bandwidth that restricts the potential flow of communications between chips. The same problem applies within a chip, which may have tens of thousands or even millions of logic elements. The need for connections between elements rises even more rapidly than the number of them, leading to congestion as the bandwidth of the fine metal deposits that serve as wires on a chip becomes saturated. One solution may be a hybrid integrated circuit, in which light carries data and program instructions to electronic transistors that do the processing. Scientists at Bell Labs long ago developed an ingredient essential to such a device. In 1965, they demon-

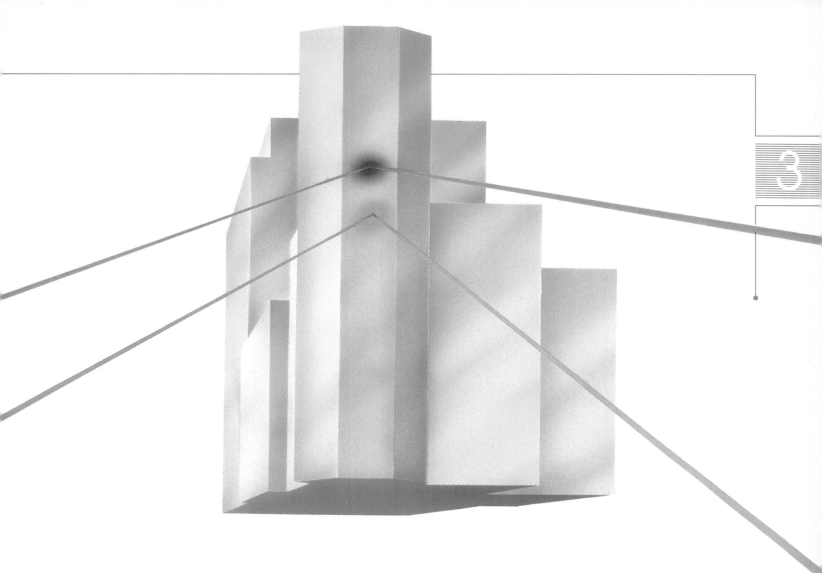

strated that fine channels could be etched into the surface of a silicon chip to serve as waveguides for light.

Instead of being channeled, of course, light can be beamed from chip to chip either directly or by reflection. Inside a chip, such an approach might solve a problem known as clock skew. Most computers march to the cadence of a high-speed clock that synchronizes their activities. The electronic pulse of this timekeeper travels so slowly that components far from the clock would fall out of step if nearer components responded as soon as the tick arrived. To solve this difficulty, nearby elements pause until the tick arrives at the more distant components. Synchronization must be accurate within about 1/100 of a clock cycle, so as computer timepieces tick faster, the margin for error becomes smaller and clock skew becomes correspondingly difficult to compensate for.

Joseph W. Goodman, professor of electrical engineering at Stanford, has been trying to solve the clock-skew problem by converting the timing signal from an electrical pulse into a flicker of light. Sent out from a centrally located laser diode, the tick of the clock would arrive virtually simultaneously at tiny photodetectors mounted wherever necessary on a chip to coordinate operations.

MORE RESPONSIBILITY FOR PHOTONS
Not only does light show promise for improving communications within electronic computers, it may someday be harnessed for the actual processing of

THE POWER OF LIGHT AND SOUND

A blue beam from an argon laser pulses through the lenses, prisms, and crystals that constitute the prototype of the first optical digital computer. Named the Systolic Acousto-Optic Binary Computer (SAOBiC), the machine was built by inventor Peter Guilfoyle in 1984 to perform matrix multiplication, a procedure in which numbers arranged checkerboard fashion are multiplied and added together. Carrying out the procedure with a pair of 1,000-number matrices requires millions of calculations; the SAOBiC could execute the operations at the rate of 500 million per second.

Guilfoyle's prototype device passed a laser beam through two large crystals of tellurium dioxide, a material that changes its index of refraction in response to sound. To one edge of each crystal were attached thirty-two electrodes, each carrying a single bit of a binary number. The presence of an electric pulse represented a one; the absence of a pulse denoted a zero. A tiny transducer at the end of each electrode converted the pulses of electricity into pulses of sound.

Traveling across the crystals in thirty-two parallel paths, the sound pulses briefly altered the index of refraction, bending the laser light toward or away from an array of photodetectors positioned at the end of the light path. As a consequence of feeding numbers into the crystals in a particular sequence, the light intensities falling on the detectors held the answer to the matrix multiplication, which was displayed digitally on the computer's monitor.

data and instructions. To cast light in this role is the aim of many dedicated researchers. Some of them have been working toward optical computers of the analog variety; others see a digital approach as more promising. Yet others are investigating hybrid machines that do part of their work digitally and part as analog computers.

In the analog world of optical computing, light intensity implies value—just as voltage levels stand for numbers in electrical analog devices. Data processing by optical analog dates from the mid-1950s and the invention of synthetic-aperture radar, a method for making detailed aerial radar pictures of the ground using a small antenna instead of the impractically large antenna that would be necessary without this technique.

In synthetic-aperture radar, an aircraft or satellite fires radar impulses at the ground. Returning echoes are displayed on a video screen and recorded on a strip of photographic film as vertical lines, one line per pulse. Strong echoes darken the film more than weak ones do, thus making light the analog for the strength of the radar returns.

Together, these vertical lines form a type of hologram, a cryptic pattern of light and dark areas that, in this case, surrender their hidden image of the earth when they are placed in a simple apparatus that passes laser light first through the hologram and then through an ingenious arrangement of special lenses. From the optical processor emerges another photographic image that reveals the terrain in fine detail.

By the end of the twentieth century, variations on the holographic image-processing theme of synthetic-aperture radar might serve as the foundation for object-recognition systems. A scanner would take in a scene—perhaps an assortment of parts to be put together on an industrial assembly line. Converted to a hologram, the scene would be examined for objects having the shape that matches one of those stored as a library of holograms within the system. Analog optical processing would, in effect, permit such a system to find in a single blink all the shapes in the scene that match the one selected from the holographic library.

When perfected, such techniques would allow assembly-line robots, for example, to quickly and reliably select the correct part for the next step of fabrication. Also on the horizon are so-called brilliant weapons, such as missiles that will be able to distinguish tanks from other vehicles on the battlefield and strike them unerringly, even though the targets' precise locations might be unknown when the missile is launched. Electronic digital computers are simply not up to object-recognition problems of this kind. As one U.S. Department of Defense engineer has observed: "Crays can solve them, but not fast enough. The solution is needed on the fly, not over the weekend."

ANALOG MATH

Performing such feats sometimes depends on executing multitudes of calculations virtually instantaneously. Although optical devices for this purpose are some years away, the science behind how they might function is well understood. Light intensities, like voltages in electronic analog computing, can be added together, subtracted, multiplied, and divided to perform prodigious feats of arithmetic. Multiplication of two numbers, for example, is easily demonstrated with a couple of sheets of fogged film. To multiply nine by ten, one film would let through a ninth of the light striking it; the other, slightly darker, would pass just a tenth of the rays hitting it. A beam of known intensity passing through the less dense of the filters would be reduced to one-ninth its original brightness. Continuing through the darker film, the attenuated beam is further dimmed so that the resulting beam is only one-ninetieth as bright as the original. Inverting the fraction gives the correct answer: ninety.

Employed in this way, a sheet of exposed film constitutes a device known as a spatial light modulator (SLM), which alters or modulates light in some fashion, depending on where a beam strikes it. In the case of the fogged film, light is dimmed equally, regardless of where it passes through the emulsion. But if the film were divided into small squares, each with a different density, a beam directed at one point would be modulated differently from a beam directed at another. By simultaneously sending a beam through each square, many pairs of numbers could be multiplied in the same instant.

A photographic SLM, of course, would be too slow for any practical analog optical computer. But many other spatial light modulators are available, changing their optical characteristics in response to various external stimuli—not just light (as with film) but also such influences as sound or voltage. For example, liquid-crystal SLMs, used in calculators and watches, darken when a voltage is applied to a section of a display; withdrawing the voltage causes the section to lighten.

Still, even the fastest spatial light modulators are relatively poky. Typically they require many milliseconds—that is, billions of picoseconds—to respond to a change in voltage or sound. Using such a device to solve problems as simple as finding the product of nine and ten would be pointless. A great many multiplications would have to be performed simultaneously for an optical multiplier to be practical.

A device to do just that is being developed by Bernard Soffer and his colleague Yuri Owechko at Hughes Research Laboratories. They have created a prototype called a Programmable Realtime Incoherent Matrix Optical (PRIMO) processor that can simultaneously multiply two arrays of thirty-two numbers—a total of more than one million calculations. Their objective is a PRIMO processor able to perform a trillion multiplications in a single second, easily outstripping the fastest electronic computers. Such speed and capacity might be useful for solving otherwise intractable signal-processing problems such as those encountered in many types of radar systems.

THE DIGITAL OPTION

Analog optical computing is well suited to image processing—such as target recognition or component selection on an assembly line—where information originates in the analog form of electromagnetic waves. In the opinion of many researchers, however, analog optical computing makes much less sense where data originates in digital or numerical form, since the information would have to be converted into analog for processing and then redigitized. Moreover, optical analog computing shares the shortcomings of electronic analog *(Chapter 1)*, sacrificing accuracy for speed. Given these limitations, optical computing's prospects would be much brightened by advances on the digital front. Not surprisingly, creating an optical digital computer has been a goal of researchers for many years.

At first, these investigations focused on mimicking digital electronics with light, which meant creating the optical equivalent of the transistor. In electronic digital computing, submicroscopic transistors built on chips of silicon do all the work. They are the on-off switches from which logic gates are assembled, and in the role of memory, they serve as repositories for the surplus of electrons that spells the difference between a one and a zero.

Transistors are also amplifiers. That is, a small voltage applied to one of the three terminals of a transistor can control the passage of a much-larger voltage between the other two terminals. Amplification is desirable in order to keep electronic pulses from fading away as they speed from point to point inside the computer. If transistors lacked amplification, it would have to be provided by some other means, which would make computers bulkier, more complex, more expensive—and slower.

Efforts toward an optical transistor began shortly after the first operation of a laser at Hughes Research Laboratories in 1960. One of the earliest proposals came from IBM physicist Alan Fowler. He availed himself of tiny lasers—as little as 300 micrometers long—made of the semiconductor gallium arsenide. Fowler's idea hinged on the observation that the beam of one such laser dimmed when the device was struck from the side by a beam from a second laser. This phenomenon, called quenching, offered the possibility of optical binary operations. Turning on the second laser would result in a dim output—a zero—from the first; switching the control laser off would yield a one.

Joined by fellow IBM physicist Gordon Lasher, Fowler published a paper in 1964 that explained mathematically how pairs or quartets of such lasers might be arranged to build logic gates and memory cells suitable for digital computing with light. But there were obstacles in the way of applying their idea. In those days, laser diodes had to be cooled in liquid nitrogen, and the lasers were inefficient. Less than one percent of the energy used to run them was converted into light; the rest was wasted as heat, which made the lasers virtually impossible to keep cool for extended periods. On top of these problems, the dimming effect of one laser on the other was at least fifty times too small. Seeing these barriers as insurmountable and eager to pursue other research, IBM abandoned the optical field in 1969.

SWITCHES AND MORE

With AT&T's invention of the room-temperature laser diode a couple of years later, the cooling problem was solved. But other difficulties arose, and several years passed before scientists at Bell Laboratories, under the direction of Peter Smith, built an optical switch around the laser diode. A version appeared in 1978 that made use of a nearly microscopic waveguide similar to those that had been etched onto silicon at Bell Labs more than a decade earlier. In place of silicon, however, Smith used a crystal of lithium niobate, a transparent quartzlike material, as the substrate or base for the waveguide, and he deposited a semireflective finish on the ends of the waveguide to make a Fabry-Perot resonator.

Invented in 1897 by French physicists Charles Fabry and Alfred Perot, the device permits an entering beam to exit only if the length is carefully tailored to the wavelength of the light sent through it. Without such pains, light waves interfere destructively—canceling each other—and little light emerges from the device. When the Fabry-Perot cell is the correct length, however, the light waves resonate—reinforcing each other through constructive interference—as they bounce between the reflective ends of the resonator. Under these circumstances, light inside the device rapidly becomes bright enough to break out.

Smith purposely made his lithium niobate Fabry-Perot waveguide too short for the wavelength of the laser he planned to shine through it, knowing that the crystal had the property of changing its index of refraction when a voltage is applied. (Refraction accounts for the bending of light beams as they pass through a lens to form an image; the index of refraction is a number that indicates the degree to which a material bends light.) To a light wave entering the resonator, altering its index of refraction is the same as changing its length enough for constructive interference to occur.

To supply the minuscule amount of electricity required, Smith diverted a tiny

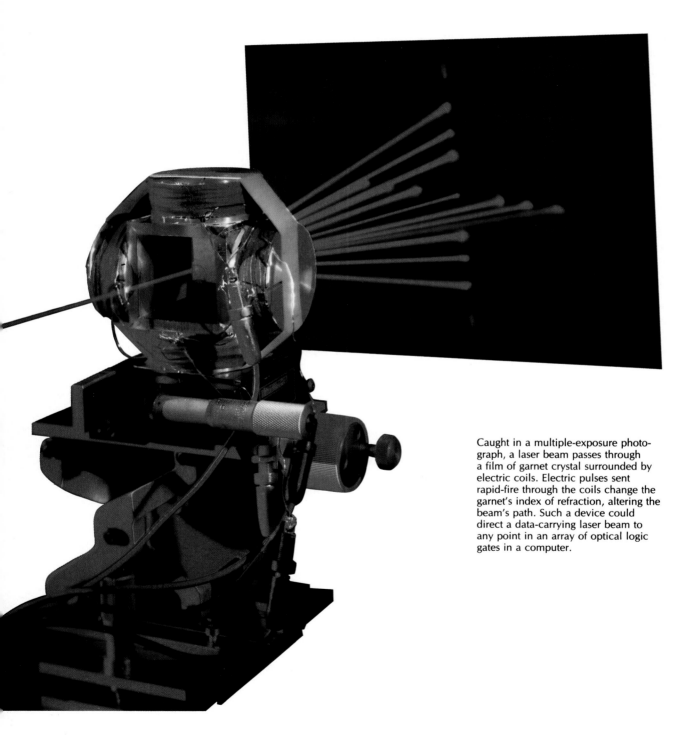

Caught in a multiple-exposure photograph, a laser beam passes through a film of garnet crystal surrounded by electric coils. Electric pulses sent rapid-fire through the coils change the garnet's index of refraction, altering the beam's path. Such a device could direct a data-carrying laser beam to any point in an array of optical logic gates in a computer.

fraction of the small quantity of light emerging from the waveguide to a photodetector, which converted the light energy contained in the intercepted rays to a voltage that was applied to the crystal. As the index of refraction changed in response to the voltage, the light beam approached a step closer to resonance. More light was converted to voltage, further altering the index of refraction. Within a few billionths of a second, Smith's device became precisely the right length for resonance, and a bright beam suddenly emerged from the waveguide. The process displayed a property called bistability: When the input beam was dimmed, the output beam remained bright until the intensity decreased well below the level at which resonance had occurred. Though as interested in the possibilities of routing lightborne telephone calls through a network as in computing, Peter Smith and his colleagues had invented a device that could also perform binary logic operations. A bright laser beam emerging from the waveguide could signify a one, while a dim beam could stand for a zero. The AT&T switch, however, offered nothing in the way of amplification.

A PHYSICS OF SUDDEN CHANGE

The lithium niobate crystal used in Bell Labs' optical switch exhibited a property called nonlinearity. One science writer has likened nonlinearity to ''a ketchup bottle. First, none'll come, then a lot'll.'' That is, when stimulated in some manner, a nonlinear material shows little or no response until the degree of stimulation passes a point called a threshold. Then the material suddenly responds sharply. In the case of lithium niobate, a dim switching beam caused no change in the index of refraction; only an intense beam produced a change.

Nonlinear behavior can enable some materials to act as amplifiers. One such material is indium antimonide. Illuminated by dim laser light, it is opaque; brighter light turns it transparent. In 1981, Professor Desmond Smith of Scotland's Heriot-Watt University exploited this nonlinearity to construct an optical transistor that he called a transphasor. Smith aimed two lasers at a crystal of indium antimonide. One beam, having an intensity just below the material's transparency threshold, shone on the crystal continuously. The second laser, which could be turned on and off, was adjusted so that the combined light of the two lasers exceeded the crystal's transparency threshold. Only with the second laser switched on would the crystal become transparent and allow the light of both lasers to pass. Inasmuch as a dim input beam controlled a bright output beam, Smith's transphasor met not only the switching criterion for a transistor, but the amplification test as well. Yet the transphasor has remained a laboratory curiosity, primarily because it, too, works only when cooled by liquid nitrogen to a temperature near absolute zero.

SEEDS OF PROGRESS

Meanwhile, scientists at Bell Laboratories persisted in their efforts to make a workable optical switch. In 1986, physicist David Miller, a former colleague of

Desmond Smith, patented a new kind of optical transistor. Called a SEED (for Self-Electro-optic Effect Device), it functions at room temperature.

SEEDs are made by alternating layers of two similar semiconductor materials—gallium arsenide and gallium aluminum arsenide. Scores of the layers, each only ten-billionths of a meter thick, are laid one atop the other by means of techniques developed for depositing ultrathin strata of silicon and other materials during the fabrication of electronic integrated circuits. This semiconductor sandwich contains free electrons that tend to gather in the gallium arsenide layers, where they remain as if trapped in a deep hole. Once they have fallen in, they cannot escape. Indeed, physicists term these layers quantum wells. Because a SEED consists of many such traps, it is called a multiple quantum well (MQW) device.

The layers of gallium arsenide in an MQW are so thin that an electron trapped there loses its identity as a particle and takes on the character of a quantum-mechanical wave that gives the MQW new properties. Among them is a curious response to a change in voltage applied to the sandwich: At low voltages, the

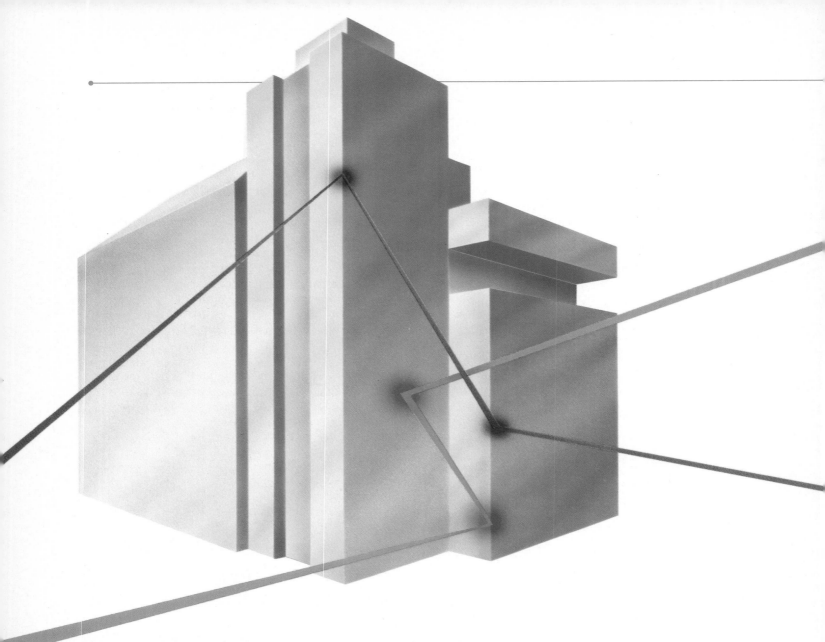

SEED is transparent, while at higher voltages it becomes opaque. One means of applying such a voltage is to illuminate the SEED with a laser, the strength of the voltage depending on the intensity of the light beam. With a sufficiently brilliant laser, the SEED turns opaque. Manipulated by two laser beams—one almost bright enough to make the SEED opaque and a second just intense enough to exceed that threshhold when combined with the first—a SEED becomes, like the transphasor, an amplifying switch. The presence or absence of a weak beam controls the passage of a much stronger one.

The promise of SEEDs prompted Bell Laboratories to intensify the effort to develop means for computing optically. In this spirit David Miller built four SEEDs on a single microchip in 1986, a modest but important step toward developing the technology needed to link large numbers of them in optical circuits. Progress has continued since then. Bell researchers have developed new types of MQW optical transistors offering switching speeds as short as two-trillionths of a second.

SEEDs and their relatives are unlikely to be employed in optical computers in the same way as transitors are most often used in electronic computers—that is, as logic gates in a von Neumann-style machine. Instead, parallel processing will be the rule. Arrays of optical transistors, perhaps numbering a million or more in a space the size of a small letter *o* on this page, will serve as logic gates or memory cells. Just as a magnifying glass focuses all the rays of an image at the same instant, simple lenses can be used in optical computing to simultaneously direct vast numbers of laser beams encoded with data or program instructions to individual logic gates or memory locations. Light also makes possible new approaches to logic that are impractical or impossible with electricity. One example is called symbolic substitution, in which patterns of light and dark squares—tiny mosaics rather than two levels of brightness—stand for ones and zeros *(pages 72-73)*.

According to proponents of this technology, moving it from the laboratory into practical computers will take the rest of the century, if not even longer. But many computer scientists are even less sanguine. Citing speed improvements in electronic computers, they doubt whether optics can ever catch up. Some believe that an optical computer is unlikely to be built unless it will be at least 100 times faster than its electronic equivalent, a goal that may be difficult to reach. In the laboratories of Japan's Nippon Telegraph and Telephone Company and Hughes Research, transistors based on electronic effects similar to the quantum wells put to use in the SEED have shown switching intervals as short as two picoseconds—that is, as fast as the optical devices that are under investigation at Bell Laboratories.

A NEW CHEMISTRY OF COMPUTING

Investigators into optical computing are operating on the near horizon compared to scientists looking into the possibility of building computers from organic molecules. Five hundred times smaller than a SEED, computing elements constructed on a molecular scale would consume less energy and, as a consequence, produce less problem-causing heat. If they ever become a reality, molecular computers could be far faster than optical devices or computers based on quantum-effect transistors.

Such ideas would hardly have been accorded a civil reception among scientists before the advances in biochemistry of the 1970s. By that time, researchers had begun to appreciate that the shape of a molecule determines how it reacts with other substances. Computer-graphics software enabled chemists to examine three-dimensional images of organic molecules from every angle and to experiment on the screen with the way those shapes fit together. In the lab, biochemists learned how to fashion such molecules from their component atoms and to create new molecules having different properties from those found in nature. Some of these scientists began to look for molecules displaying characteristics that might be adapted to computing.

In the early 1970s, chemist Ari Aviram of IBM collaborated with Mark Ratner at New York University to develop a theory of molecular rectifiers, electronic components that convert the alternating

In Pursuit of the Molecular Computer

Biochemists have known since the 1930s that chemicals present in the human body—proteins, enzymes, peptides, and a host of others—interact largely because of their shapes and electrical charges. Each molecule has a uniquely configured peg that fits a matching hole in another molecule. This principle holds the answers to questions of disease and health—how viruses destroy cells, for example, and how antibodies, the body's natural defense against invading organisms, overcome the viruses.

Computer scientists have recognized in these biomedical revelations the potential for a new kind of computer made of biochips, molecule assemblages intended to be grown through a sequence of chemical reactions that fit one mol-

Skimming the Surface

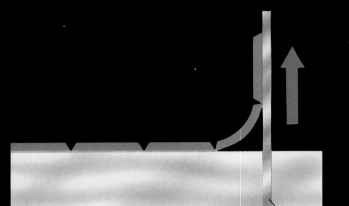

Protein Molecule

Seen here in cross section, a layer of protein molecules one molecule thick floats on water. Electrical charges on the proteins link them together in a film having all the component molecules oriented in the same direction.

Silicon

A thin sheet, usually of silicon, is dipped into the tank and then withdrawn (above), transferring the protein film from the surface of the water to the silicon. The molecules in the film become the foundation for a biochip (right).

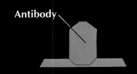

Antibody

A monoclonal antibody attaches to a protein molecule, the first step in erecting the structures that will support the chip's computing elements.

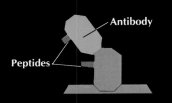

Antibody

Peptides

In separate immersions, a second monoclonal antibody attaches to the first, then both antibodies accept identical peptides. Additional peptides are attached if the computing element needs more than two anchor points.

Computing Element

With the peptides serving as hooks, the emerging structure can now hold a computing element, capable of serving as a logic gate or memory cell.

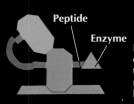

Peptide

Enzyme

In preparation for linking the computing elements electrically, a third peptide attaches to the lower monoclonal antibody and becomes host to an enzyme.

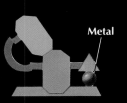

Metal

Reacting with other chemicals, the enzyme deposits a spot of metal. Only a few hundred atoms wide, the metal serves as an electrical path for program instructions or data.

ecule to another, peg into perfectly fitting hole. Even man-made molecules called monoclonal antibodies, taken out of their usual role as cancer-fighting agents, could become parts of biochips.

A likely first step in constructing a biochip is to float a film of protein molecules a single molecule thick on the surface of water in a tank. By a method known as the Langmuir-Blodgett technique, the array of proteins would be transferred from the water surface to a supporting sheet of silicon or quartz *(far left)*. The plan then is to dip the sheet of protein molecules into a succession of tanks, each containing a chip component in solution.

Step-by-step, the component molecules would attach themselves to the proteins and to each other simultaneously, creating millions of identical logic gates or memory cells, depending on the type of molecular computing element attached to them *(pages 100-103)*.

In either case, a biochip would accept input and express output by means of laser light. Projecting a laser beam fine enough to strike a single computing element of such a chip has been a major obstacle to a practical biocomputer. Efforts to design tiny photodetectors to sense the laser output have been equally frustrating. So far, the most promising solution is to make many neighboring elements act as one so that laser beams and photodetectors could be larger than would be permitted if each element were addressed individually.

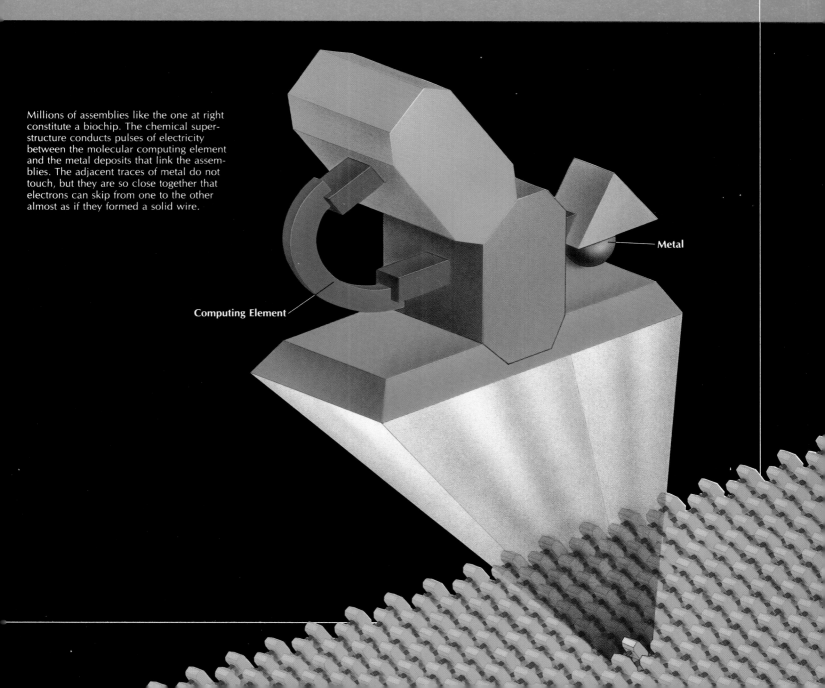

Millions of assemblies like the one at right constitute a biochip. The chemical super-structure conducts pulses of electricity between the molecular computing element and the metal deposits that link the assemblies. The adjacent traces of metal do not touch, but they are so close together that electrons can skip from one to the other almost as if they formed a solid wire.

Metal

Computing Element

A Logical Assembly of Molecules

A promising candidate for the role of logic element in biochips is the wishbone arrangement of molecules shown below, comprised of four types of molecules in all. Individually, they are unexceptional. Two of them, members of the cyanine and polyene families of molecules, are dyes that are used in color photography. A third type, quinone, is taken from plants and bacteria, where it serves in the process of photosynthesis. A porphyrin molecule carries oxygen in the bloodstream. A collection of atoms called a sigma group is a kind of molecular glue.

When joined together, however, these modest components form a structure having electrical and optical properties that make it suitable for use as a logic gate, one of the tiny circuits that permit a computer to execute complex instructions. Spe-

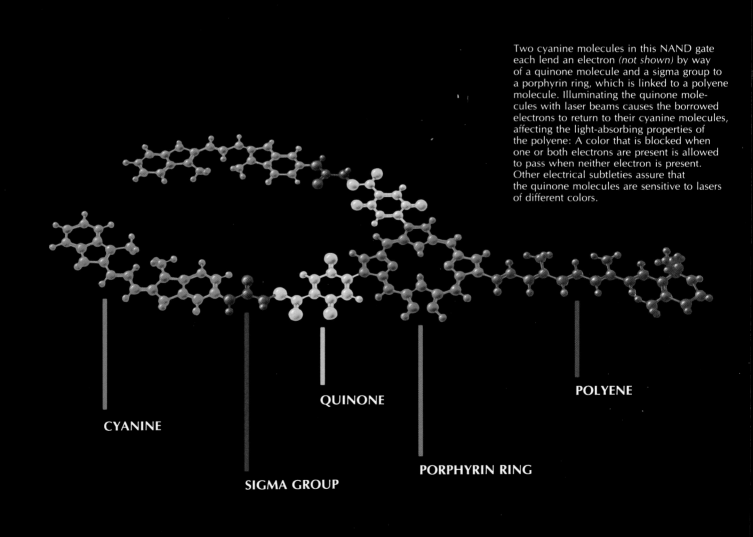

Two cyanine molecules in this NAND gate each lend an electron (not shown) by way of a quinone molecule and a sigma group to a porphyrin ring, which is linked to a polyene molecule. Illuminating the quinone molecules with laser beams causes the borrowed electrons to return to their cyanine molecules, affecting the light-absorbing properties of the polyene: A color that is blocked when one or both electrons are present is allowed to pass when neither electron is present. Other electrical subtleties assure that the quinone molecules are sensitive to lasers of different colors.

CYANINE

SIGMA GROUP

QUINONE

PORPHYRIN RING

POLYENE

cifically, this assembly of molecules functions as a NAND gate. A logic gate (the others are named AND, NOT, OR, and XOR) is known by its inputs and outputs. In the case of a NAND gate, the output is a zero only if both of its two inputs are ones. Any other combination of ones and zeros as inputs yields a one as the output.

NAND gates can be wired together to perform the functions of all the others. This unique feature permits a versatile computer logic to be created from a single type of logic gate, a necessary simplicity if an array of logic elements is to be assembled using the process explained on the preceding pages. Yet NAND-gate logic requires up to three times as many logic elements as would be necessary if other types of gates were also used. Such a large number of logic elements would slow a conventional, silicon-based computer considerably. But in a biocomputer, this weakness would be more than overcome by the phenomenal speed of molecular logic elements, which promise to be a thousand times faster than identical gates made of silicon.

Inputs for this molecular NAND gate take the form of laser light beamed at the quinone molecules. Subtleties in the distribution of electrons (not seen at the scale of these illustrations) among the gate's molecules make each of the two quinone molecules sensitive to light of different colors, thereby permitting each input to be addressed unambiguously. Output is a third laser beam that the gate, depending on the inputs, either blocks or permits to reach a detector, thus expressing either a zero or a one.

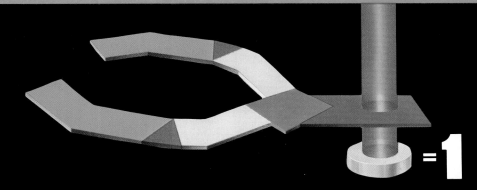

In this simplified drawing of the NAND gate, both inputs are zeros. That is, neither quinone molecule *(yellow)* is illuminated by a laser beam. Under these circumstances, the polyene molecule *(purple)* allows the red beam of an output laser to reach a detector, signaling a one as the NAND gate's output.

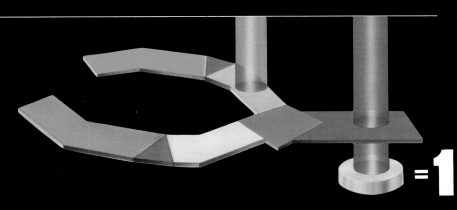

To produce inputs of one and zero, a laser may be shone on either quinone molecule. In this instance, the upper quinone is illuminated, forcing an electron from the porphyrin ring to the upper cyanine molecule *(light green)*. However, the absence of a single electron from the porphyrin ring has an insignificant effect on the color sensitivity of the polyene molecule. The output laser reaches the detector, and the gate yields a one.

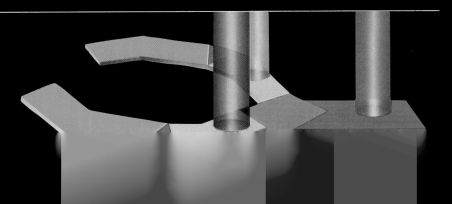

With a laser beam striking each quinone molecule, both inputs to the gate are ones, and both borrowed electrons in the porphyrin ring return to their cyanine molecules. The absence of the two electrons changes the color sensitivity of the polyene molecule sufficiently to block the output laser beam. No light reaches the detector, signifying a zero as the gate's output.

A Light-Sensitive Protein for Memory

A bacterium that grows in the salt marshes near California's Silicon Valley contains a protein that researchers believe can serve as the memory element in a biochip. Called bacteriorhodopsin, the protein is similar to the human protein rhodopsin (visual purple), the molecule in the eye's retina that converts light into a nerve impulse.

Bacteriorhodopsin, which converts light into chemical energy, has a useful characteristic: Its chemical structure is modified when it is exposed to red or green light *(below, left)*. The change wrought by light of one color is permanent—unless it is reversed by the influence of the other color. This feature is tailor-made for computer memory, which

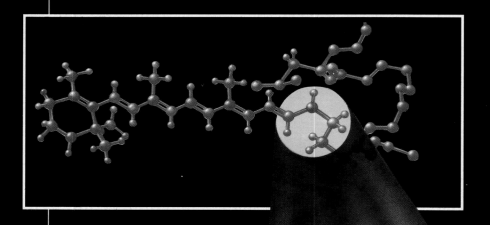

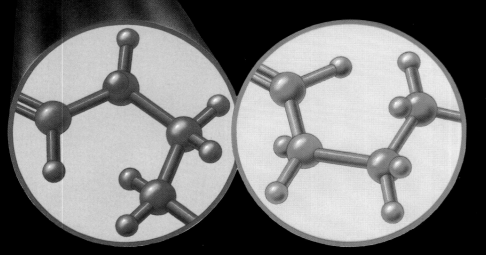

A horseshoe arrangement of atoms within the bacteriorhodopsin molecule flips from one orientation to another when the molecule is exposed to colored laser light. A brief exposure to red light turns the open side of the horseshoe downward; green light flips the open side upward.

stores data as sequences of zeros and ones, or, in this instance, reds and greens.

The state of the molecule—that is, whether it has most recently been exposed to red or green light—is easy to detect. In the red state, the molecule is opaque to all colors of light except red; in the green state, only green light can get through. Either color might be used to read the memory, except for the tendency of green light to change red cells (zeros) to green (ones) and vice versa, altering memory contents even as they are examined. A solution to this dilemma, a problem called destructive readout, is a composite red-and-green laser beam for reading the memory (below, right).

Reading a Molecule's Memory

A read beam of laser light, half red and half green, flashes through a bacteriorhodopsin molecule encoded with a zero by previous exposure to red light. In this state, the molecule blocks the green half of the beam while passing the red half to a photodetector. Sensing the color of the light as red, the detector instantly turns off the green half of the beam, preventing it from flipping the molecule into the green, or one, state. Then the detector transmits an electric pulse signifying a zero.

When encoded with a one by exposure to green light, a bacteriorhodopsin molecule passes only the green half of the read beam to the photodetector. Under these circumstances, the detector first turns off the red half of the beam to preserve the data stored in the molecule, then sends a pulse that represents a one.

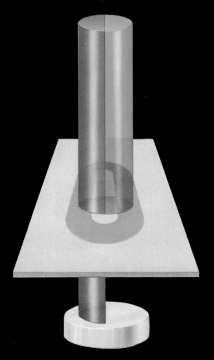

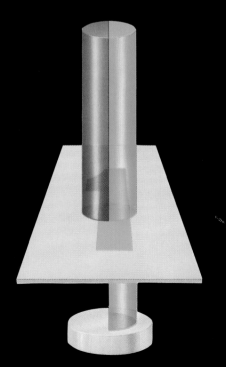

plus and minus voltages of alternating current to the positive value of direct current. The two researchers were also able to synthesize a number of molecules that are electrically bistable—equally content to be either positively or negatively charged (most molecules prefer one state to the other). These bistable molecules could be switched between the states simply by applying a voltage, making the molecules potential candidates for use as binary memory units or switches. Casting about for other molecules that might show useful electronic properties, the scientists in 1974 put together an organic sandwich that functioned as a diode, an electronic component that prevents backflow of current through a circuit.

Aviram and Ratner's organic diode consisted of a chemical called TTF that readily gives up electrons, a second chemical called TCNQ that takes on extra electrons, and an intermediate layer of octane, the substance used to improve the burning qualities of gasoline. Arrangements of atoms within these three molecules permitted electrons to flow through the octane from TTF to the TCNQ, but not in the opposite direction. Aviram and coworkers at IBM acquired a patent

on their organic diode in 1976. By then, however, development of the device had already stalled, in part because advances toward molecular switches and memory cells had not kept pace.

MOLECULAR LOGIC GATES

Interest in molecular computing revived in the next decade as advances in biotechnology provided clues to how additional components might be made and assembled. At Carnegie-Mellon University in Pittsburgh, for example, chemistry professor Robert Birge began designing computer-logic gates and high-speed memory cells made from organic compounds. One molecular assembly, shaped somewhat like a lobster's claw, would function as a NAND gate—a logic element that has two input channels and a single output channel. A binary one comes out of a NAND gate unless both inputs are ones; in that case, the output becomes a zero. Networks made exclusively of NAND gates can be used to build adders and any other computer-logic component *(pages 100-101)*.

Pursuing his work at Syracuse University's Center for Molecular Electronics, Birge has worked out a design in which forty-eight molecular gates would link together to form a one-bit adder, a building block for an arithmetic unit that would carry out high-speed calculations. Adders and other components of Birge's molecular computer would be stacked in layers of organic sensors, logic gates, and memory units; input at the top surface would work its way down through the layers, emerging as a result at the bottom, where it would be sent off to other molecular processors.

Birge's memory medium is a purple, light-sensitive protein called bacterio-rhodopsin. Under most circumstances, this chemical is transparent to red light. However, after it is exposed to green light for as short a time as three pico-seconds, bacteriorhodopsin becomes opaque to red and remains so until it is reilluminated with red light *(pages 102-103)*. Birge recognized that these properties could constitute a superior method for storing information. A red-transparent spot, for example, could represent a binary zero; a red-opaque spot would then signify a one. Red and green lasers could be used to read and write information on the surface. Spread evenly over a quartz disk, says Birge, bacteriorhodopsin could become the foundation for a random-access, optical memory that "can store and retrieve information at least one thousand times faster than current silicon memory chips."

BIOCHIPS

Except for bacteriorhodopsin's application as a form of memory, Birge's NAND gate and memory cells would be useless to computing without some method of linking them together. A theory of how this might be accomplished has been proposed by two U.S. scientists, biophysicist James McAlear and electrical engineer John Wehrung. Although their work has produced no biochips, it has earned the cautious approval of colleagues. Alwyn Scott, a physicist at the University of Arizona, Tucson, notes that "our understanding of biological materials as construction tools is roughly similar to our knowledge of semiconductors in, say, 1935. I have a lot of respect for what they're doing."

An important building block of McAlear and Wehrung's hypothetical biochip is a monoclonal antibody, a genetically engineered molecule that can be grown by the millions. Designed to bind with other molecules at specific sites, the antibodies would become part of a framework that could support computing elements—such as Birge's memory cells and NAND gates—and link them together. Arrays consisting of millions of such computing elements could be constructed simultaneously simply by dipping a piece of supporting material such as silicon into a succession of baths containing the molecular chip components (pages 98-99). Each memory cell or logic gate would be so minuscule as to make wiring them together into a computer impossible. So McAlear and Wehrung have proposed ultrafine laser beams, of wavelengths carefully tailored to the particular molecules in a chip, as a means of both input and output.

McAlear and Wehrung have as yet built no such structure. However, if they or Birge —or some other molecular-computing enthusiast—were to accomplish this feat, the results might be nothing short of astounding: "From the first integrated circuits in 1958 to the present," says McAlear, "the reduction in the dimension circuits has been a thousandfold—submillimeter to submicron. The difference between that and the limits of molecular circuits is another thousandfold reduction—submicron to subnanometer. Computer capability at these new limits would be one million times as powerful as today's machines."

As alluring as this technology may appear, mountainous obstacles stand between the concepts and a working computer. Robert Clerman of the MITRE Corporation, a research firm with headquarters near Boston, Massachusetts, maintains that "classical organic synthesis is not going to be sufficient to successfully fabricate molecular-scale systems." In order to put together a biochip, Clerman believes, a great deal more needs to be learned about the three-dimensional structure of molecules and about the way molecules fit together. Breakthroughs in the fields of chemistry and biology will be necessary.

Yet even if the necessary insights were gained tomorrow, fundamental questions would arise over how molecular computers might function best. One possibility might be to emulate the serial, digital electronic machines of the present, their organic molecules simply taking the place of semiconductor crys-

Physicist Richard Feynman, a Nobel laureate and legendary teacher, holds forth in a classroom at Caltech. Three decades ago, Feynman's fascination with subatomic particles led him to speculate that technological miniaturization could proceed right down to the atomic scale, with small machines being used to build still-smaller machines until the limits of matter had been reached.

Eric Drexler contemplates a model of a molecule, a player in his scenario for atomic-level engineering. Reversing Feynman's concept of progressive miniaturization, Drexler envisions tiny, computerized devices building colossal edifices, one atom at a time.

tals. On the other hand, computing with proteins might take an optical turn. Or perhaps, as Robert Birge suggests, there will emerge some inherent capacity that leads to an entirely new form of computer.

TOWARD NANOTECHNOLOGY

Considering the challenges that confront the development of a computer technology on the molecular frontier, the idea of logic gates or memory cells on an atomic scale would seem to be pure fantasy. Yet no less an authority than the late Nobel Prize-winning physicist Richard Feynman raised just such a prospect when he said in 1959 that "the principles of physics do not speak against the possibility of maneuvering things atom by atom. It would be possible, in principle, for a physicist to synthesize any chemical substance that the chemist writes down."

Feynman saw the manipulation of individual atoms as a natural—perhaps inevitable—extension of science and technology. He noted that the first machines, large and crude, were used to build smaller and finer machines. They, in turn, were used to construct still smaller and finer devices, and so on until, by the time Feynman rendered his opinion of atomic construction, it was clear that electronic devices would soon shrink to a near-microscopic scale. Logic suggested that this shrinkage of tools will continue until the limits of matter are reached—the atoms that distinguish one element from another.

Feynman's expected evolution of machines building ever-smaller machines became known as the top-down approach. Twenty years later, Eric Drexler, then an engineer at M.I.T., concluded that molecular engineering would make it possible to work "from the bottom up"—to use molecule-size tools to construct larger machines. "Atoms and molecules are the ultimate building components," says Drexler, "an engineer's heaven."

By Drexler's reasoning, virtually any kind of mechanism that is built on a large scale can be constructed on an atomic scale once we understand how to manipulate atoms individually. He chose the term *nanotechnology* to describe this engineering heaven, and he and a growing band of fellow scientists set to work examining where it might lead.

Nanomachines will be "engines of abundance," says Drexler, invoking nature's own achievements. "Teams of nanomachines in nature build whales, and seeds replicate machinery and organize atoms into vast structures of cellulose, building redwood trees." That being so, "there is nothing too startling about growing a rocket engine in a specially prepared vat. Indeed, foresters given suitable assembler 'seeds' could grow spaceships from soil, air, and sunlight."

FRAGILE MACHINES

Nanotechnology's first creations, of necessity, must be more modest. The chemicals of life are not materials from which rocket engines or machinery can be made. Such molecules tend to come apart when heated, fracture when frozen, and crumble when dried. As Drexler observes, "We do not build machines of flesh. We use our hands of flesh to build machines of wood, ceramic, steel, and plastic." As a consequence, he says, "We will use protein machines to build nanomachines of tougher stuff than protein."

First, proteins might fit themselves together to serve as intermediary machines, called assemblers, which might be grown to order from protein soups of various ingredients. A crew of these nanoconstructors, perhaps having arms that could be programmed to select and grasp molecules or atoms of other substances, would assemble tougher nanoconstructor offspring of carbon. Bonded in different ways, atoms of this element could either form flexible, tough layers of diamond fiber or rods of a graphitelike material sliding almost friction-free within diamond channels. This second generation of assemblers would in turn build more advanced machines that could be sent to work, equipped with the molecular blueprints for a huge project. On the job site, furnished with a stew of building materials, the machines will select molecules and stack them as called for in the plans.

Such programmed autonomy conjures nightmares of a runaway technology. Drexler himself points out that a "gray goo" of malignant nanomachines could be designed to multiply and gobble up every living thing on earth. Even if no one loosed such a scourge, it is easy to imagine other consequences. For example, consider the chaos that would be wrought by a nanoconstruction crew misprogrammed to build not one skyscraper, but an endless series of them.

Even as chemists ponder the techniques and consequences of molecular assembly, other questions lurk in the background. The smallest particles of matter do not remain stationary; ways must be devised to prevent their vibrations from impeding precision. Molecular activity produces heat. It must be removed before it can destroy the nanomachines, which would also need protection from radiation that could disrupt chemical bonds and cause malfunctions.

Eric Drexler's nanoworld lies at the bottom of the chart at right, which compares approximate metric dimensions of objects as scientists often do—by orders of magnitude or powers of ten. From any level on the chart, one step upward is ten times (one order of magnitude) larger; a step down represents an order-of-magnitude decrease in size.

POWER	METRIC	EXAMPLE
10^{10} 10,000,000,000	10 gigameters	diameter of the red giant star Antares
10^9 1,000,000,000	1 gigameter	diameter of the Sun
10^8 100,000,000	100 megameters	diameter of Saturn
10^7 10,000,000	10 megameters	distance from North Pole to equator
10^6 1,000,000	1 megameter	distance from New York to Chicago
10^5 100,000	100 kilometers	width of Lake Erie
10^4 10,000	10 kilometers	half the length of Manhattan Island
10^3 1,000	1 kilometer	twelve city blocks
10^2 100	100 meters	thirty-story skyscraper
10^1 10	1 dekameter	house with an attic
10^0 1	1 meter	four-year-old child
10^{-1} 0.1	1 decimeter	width of the human hand
10^{-2} 0.01	1 centimeter	mosquito
10^{-3} 0.001	1 millimeter	flea
10^{-4} 0.0001	100 microns	grain of sand
10^{-5} 0.00001	10 microns	paramecium
10^{-6} 0.000001	1 micron	human sperm cell (minus tail)
10^{-7} 0.0000001	100 nanometers	gene
10^{-8} 0.00000001	10 nanometers	hemoglobin molecule
10^{-9} 0.000000001	1 nanometer	sugar molecule
10^{-10} 0.0000000001	1 angstrom	hydrogen atom

Ever optimistic, nanotechnologists are confident that they will overcome these and other obstacles, just as similar problems have been solved in nature. Although doing so will be a decades-long challenge, the benefits anticipated from nanoengineering would be stupendous. Nanocomputers no bigger than a bacterium might be capable of operating thousands of times faster than today's supercomputers. Such tiny computers could direct healing machines far smaller than a single cell or could become part of a diamond-fiber spacesuit as sensitive as skin and tougher than steel. Gangs of assemblers could build huge edifices and even artificial worlds in space in such a way that they would seem to materialize from nothing *(pages 111-119)*.

As remote as nanotechnological marvels may seem, they square with the history of science. One of the most prescient forecasters of future technology was the thirteenth-century philosopher Roger Bacon, whose work in optics gave Europeans their first inkling of the microscopic world. Bacon lived at a time when the discipline of science was still new and largely untested, and when most of its possibilities were unimagined by all but a few. As if to warn future generations against an excess of skepticism, Bacon wrote: "Science concerns the fabrication of instruments such as machines for flying, or for moving in vehicles without animals and yet with incomparable speed, or of navigating without oarsmen more swiftly. Incredible weights can be raised or lowered without difficulty or labor. Also machines can be made for walking in the sea and the rivers, even to the bottom, without danger."

Bacon had less idea of how these things might be accomplished than Drexler has of the route to nanotechnology, yet everything that the medieval philosopher foretold has come to pass. Perhaps that is the reason why not even skeptics debate the arrival of nanotechnology, only the timetable.

Into the Nanoworld

- *On a quiet city street corner, empty of workmen and machinery, a gleaming skyscraper takes shape in a single day.*
- *A child, critically injured in a traffic accident, is healed from within by an army of microscopic medical drones.*
- *A village blighted by crop failure is saved by converting straw and dirt into food and drink.*

Such prospective wonders, once ventured only in the most fanciful science fiction, may become possible through an emerging field of engineering called nanotechnology. (From the Greek word for dwarf, *nano* signifies one-billionth in the scientific world.) "With our present technology we are still forced to handle atoms in unruly herds," explains research engineer Eric Drexler, a leading thinker in the field. "Nanotechnology will be based on molecular machines and molecular electronic devices. It will enable the construction of almost anything, building up structures atom by atom."

Within fifty years, Drexler believes, computerized, robot-like nanomachines called assemblers will be able to link atoms into virtually any structure. These assemblers—so small that their surfaces would be knobby with atoms—would be able to replicate themselves, creating armies of molecule-size builders capable of carrying out construction projects on a human scale.

However remote Drexler's notions may seem, he is confident that his vision for future technology is inevitable. "The laws of nature leave plenty of room for progress," he says. "The greatest technological breakthrough in history is yet to come." Examples of what he foresees—microcomputing in its most literal sense—appear on the following pages.

Automatons for a New Medicine

Floating inside the nucleus of a human cell, an assembler-built repair vessel performs some genetic maintenance. Stretching a supercoil of DNA between its lower pair of robot arms, the nanomachine gently pulls the unwound strand through an opening in its prow for analysis. Upper arms, meanwhile, detach regulatory proteins from the chain and place them in an intake port. The molecular structures of both DNA and proteins are compared to information stored in the database of a larger nanocomputer positioned outside the nucleus and connected to the cell-repair ship by a communications link. Irregularities found in either structure are corrected and the proteins reattached to the DNA chain, which re-coils into its original form.

That such medical wizardry may one day be possible is perhaps the most dramatic illustration of the revolutionary potential of nanotechnology. With a diameter of only fifty nanometers, the repair vessel would be smaller than most bacteria and viruses, yet capable of therapies and cures well beyond the reach of present-day physicians. With trillions of these self-replicating machines coursing through a patient's bloodstream, "internal medicine" would take on new significance. Disease would be attacked at the molecular level, and such maladies as cancer, viral infections, and arteriosclerosis could be wiped out. An ability to regenerate new living tissue would make artificial organs and transplants unnecessary. In time, through the repair of damaged cells and correction of chemical imbalances, the very process of aging might be arrested.

Engines Made
from Soup

Nanomachines, in the opinion of Eric Drexler, will be the builders of tomorrow. As just one example of the sort of work these devices might do, he describes the creation of a rocket engine in a huge vat.

First, a nanocomputer "seed" containing the plans and technical data for a rocket engine is placed in the vat. A flick of a switch floods the chamber with a viscous liquid containing trillions of assembler nanomachines, each equipped with an on-board computer. Assemblers adhere to the nano-seed and begin plugging themselves together layer upon layer, following directions issued by the central nanocomputer to form a delicate latticework.

Soon a translucent, engine-shaped skeleton emerges. The vat is then flushed with liquid to carry away unneeded assemblers and heat that they have generated. A new fluid brings in dissolved compounds, which the remaining assem-blers break down to release aluminum and carbon. Swarming over the chambers of a honeycomb scaffolding, the assemblers operate in unison, as if an army of human construction workers were performing identical tasks in a series of identical rooms of a modern-day skyscraper. For areas needing high strength, the assemblers bond carbon molecules from the surrounding liquid to form diamond fiber. For resistance to heat and corrosion, sapphire strands are made by combining oxygen and aluminum.

As the assemblers finish their work, they escape into the fluid wash, sealing up their escape channels behind them. In their wake stands a gleaming, lightweight, seamless rocket engine. The entire project has taken less than a day, and to the human eye, incapable of detecting the microscopic building crew, the engine appears to have sprung up from nothing, like rock candy growing on a string.

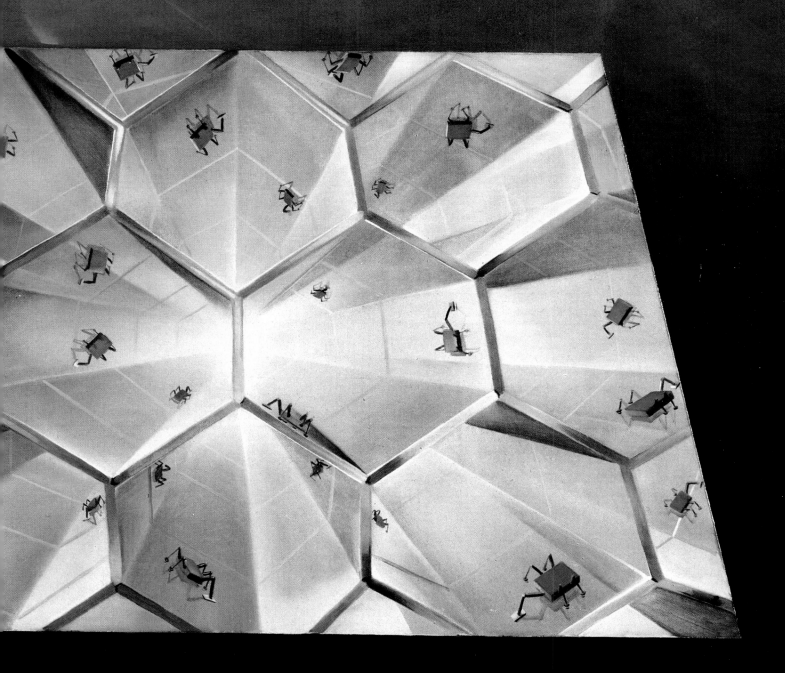

A Mechanical Fabric

Aided by the sophisticated nanostructure of his spacesuit, an astronaut in orbit near a planetoid in the frigid vacuum of space works as comfortably and freely as if in a basement workshop on earth. Fabric for the lightweight suit is a diamond-fiber weave with a structure as intricate, in its own way, as that of human skin. Each ten-micron length of fiber contains a cube-shaped nanocomputer mated to a cylindrical electric motor. Sensitive to every strain, the nanocomputers direct the motors to turn a screw inside each hollow thread, lengthening or shortening the fibers to accommodate the wearer's movements.

Trillions of nanocomputers make the suit self-repairing and programmable to various environments. The suit becomes thin at the gloves—where pressure sensors allow fingertip sensitivity—while the fabric remains thick at the arms and torso where extra protection for the wearer is needed. With a change in programming, the suit serves as artificial muscle that is capable of giving the space explorer superhuman strength.

A small backpack contains air and food supplies, but nanotechnology enables the suit to keep its occupant alive even when these provisions have been exhausted. Assemblers use sunlight to convert exhaled carbon dioxide into fresh oxygen, while other systems break down digestive wastes into simple molecules and reassemble them as food. Within this self-contained ecosystem, space travelers might one day survive and function in the hostile reaches of space for weeks or months at a time.

Outposts in Space

Floating in a remote corner of the solar system, a huge space station is ready for occupancy. One thousand kilometers in diameter, the artificial satellite is large enough to provide an earthlike environment for millions of colonists. Standing with their heads toward the center of the slowly spinning cylinder, inhabitants will feel the reassuring tug of gravity. There are mountains and valleys inside this world, thunderstorms and sunshine, and, near the center of the cylinder, an inner space where the atmosphere becomes too thin to support life.

Construction would have begun months earlier, with the arrival of a sporelike object on an asteroid's surface. Perhaps as small as a grain of sand, the spore contained a seed nano-computer, programmed with blueprints for the project, and a starter work force of a few hundred thousand assemblers.

Like the seed of a tree, the nanocomputer-driven system put out roots that burrowed into the asteroid to tap its stores of carbon, iron, nickel, cobalt, and silicates. Assemblers combined the minerals into different materials that the nanomachines used to extend the root system while simultaneously sending out a spreading array of leaflike solar collectors to intercept energy from the sun. Replicating themselves, the assemblers became an astronomical population, elaborating the root system to encircle the asteroid and enlarging the field of solar collectors until it covered an area of more than a billion square kilometers. With supplies of power and raw materials well established, the assemblers then went to work on their real task—building a self-sufficient world that, like other immense satellites created the same way, will extend the presence of humankind farther into the beckoning immensity of the universe.

Glossary

Algorithm: a set of clearly defined rules and instructions for the solution of a problem. A computer program consists of the step-by-step procedures of an algorithm.

Analog: the representation of a continuously changing physical variable (temperature, for example) by another variable (such as an electric current).

Analog computer: a computer in which data is represented by continuous physical variables such as the magnitude of voltage, rather than by the discrete on-off pulses that are used in digital computers.

AND gate: a logic circuit whose output is TRUE (or one) only when all inputs are TRUE. *See also* Logic gate.

Architecture: the design of a computer system, including both its hardware configuration and software strategies for handling data and running programs. *See also* Von Neumann architecture.

Artificial intelligence (AI): the ability of a machine to perform functions that are normally associated with human intelligence, such as comprehending spoken language, making judgments, and learning.

Assembler: a hypothetical molecular machine that could be programmed to build any molecular structure or device from simpler chemical building blocks. *See also* Nanotechnology.

Associative memory: a machine's ability to recall an entire set of data when given only a part; a capability of one type of neural network.

Astrolabe: the earliest analog computer; a device for making astronomical calculations.

Axon: the impulse-transmitting fiber of a nerve cell; the part of a neural network that emulates its function.

Back-propagation algorithm: the formula by which a neural-network computer calculates how close it has come to a correct response and adjusts the strengths of relationships between its neurons to improve its performance. *See also* Connection weights.

Backward error propagation: a process in neural-network computing whereby the computer learns from its mistakes. *See also* Back-propagation algorithm.

Bacteriorhodopsin: a purple light-sensitive protein used to create an ultrafast, high-capacity optical digital storage disk.

Bandwidth: the range of frequencies occupied by an information-bearing signal or accommodated by a transmission medium such as copper wires, microwaves, or optical fibers. The wider the bandwidth, the more data that can be transmitted.

Binary: having two components or possible states; usually represented by a code of zeros and ones.

Binary code: a system for representing things by combinations of two symbols, such as one and zero, TRUE or FALSE, or the presence or absence of light or voltage.

Binary notation: a number system that uses two as its base and expresses numbers as strings of zeros and ones. Information in a digital computer is processed and stored in binary form.

Biochip: a hypothetical device for molecular computing, which would be "grown" from organic substances, analogous to an electronic integrated circuit.

Bistability: the property that allows a material to maintain either of two opposite states (a positive or negative charge, for example) without external aid; most substances are naturally stable in only one state.

Bit: a contraction of "binary digit," the smallest unit of information in a binary computer, represented by a zero or a one.

Capacitor: a device for storing an electric charge.

Central processing unit (CPU): the part of a von Neumann computer that interprets and executes instructions; it is composed of a processor, a control unit, and a small amount of memory.

Compressed-time simulation: a computerized re-creation in which events take place more quickly than they do in reality.

Connection weights: the strengths of relationships between neurons in a neural-network computer.

Differential equation: a mathematical equation describing the interaction of a function and its rate of change. It is frequently used to model processes in the physical world.

Digital: pertaining to the representation, manipulation, or transmission of information by discrete, or on-off, signals.

Digital computer: any computer that operates on data expressed in discrete form, such as the ones and zeros of binary notation.

Digital electronic computer: a digital computer that represents and processes data electronically.

Digital optical computer: a digital computer that uses light to represent and process data.

Diode: a component of an electronic circuit that permits the current to flow in only one direction. *See also* Laser diode.

DNA (deoxyribonucleic acid): a molecule, shaped like a double helix, carrying all the genetic information necessary for the creation of an organism.

Error back propagation: *See* Backward error propagation.

Exclusive-OR gate: a logic circuit with two inputs, whose output is TRUE if either input is TRUE, but not if both of them are TRUE. *See also* Logic gate.

Flight simulator: a computerized training and testing device, programmed to respond to control movements and flight conditions as if it were a real airplane, allowing a pilot to "fly" an aircraft and examine its behavior without leaving the ground.

Fourier transform: a mathematical technique for analyzing complex phenomena, such as sound or light waves, by resolving them into their individual components.

Fuzzy data: inexact information that is difficult to convert into the digital form required by conventional computers, but for which analog computers are often well suited. "About 40" is an example of fuzzy data.

Gallium arsenide: a semiconductor material, one use of which is the fabrication of extremely small lasers.

Hologram: the recording of a three-dimensional image created by the reflection of monochromatic, coherent light (usually generated by a laser) from an object. Holograms have also been produced through the use of sound waves and microwaves.

Hopfield net: a type of neural network designed by physicist John Hopfield to solve optimization problems.

Hybrid computer: a computer that combines digital and analog techniques for manipulating data.

Input: information fed into a computer or any component.

Integrated circuit (IC): an electronic circuit whose components are formed on a single piece of semiconductor material, usually silicon; also called a chip.

Integrator: a circuit or device in a computer essential to the solution of differential analyses. *See also* Differential equation.

Interconnection: a communication channel that transmits data between computers or their components.

Laser: the acronym for Light Amplification by Stimulated Emission of Radiation; a light source that produces intense monochromatic, coherent light in a very narrow directional beam.

Laser diode: a diode that acts as a laser.

Liquid crystal (LC): a liquid with optical properties similar to those of a crystal. For example, one type of LC can be switched from opaque to transparent by an electric current, making it useful in computer displays and as a memory unit in optical computers. *See also* Spatial light modulator.

Logic gate: a circuit that accepts one or more inputs and produces a single, predictable output. *See also* AND gate; NAND gate; NOR gate; OR gate; Exclusive-OR gate; NOT gate.

Magneto-optic spatial light modulator: a device in which a magnetic field modulates, or alters, the characteristics of a beam of light. *See also* Spatial light modulator.

Memory: the principal area within a computer for storing instructions and data.

Molecular computer: a computer whose functioning components are either individual or small groups of molecules.

NAND gate: a logic gate whose output is TRUE (one), unless all its inputs are TRUE. *See also* Logic gate.

Nano: from the Greek word for dwarf; a prefix denoting the one-billionth part.

Nanocomputer: a hypothetical computer constructed by assembling individual atoms and molecules, each of which would be functional components.

Nanotechnology: theoretical processes and techniques based on the manipulation of individual atoms and molecules.

Neural network: a computer or a program modeled after the interaction of neurons in the brain, including their ability to improve performance through experience.

Neurons: nerve cells; the circuits in a computer that mimic their operation.

Nonlinearity: behavior whereby a property of a material (its transparency, for example) changes abruptly at some threshold level of stimulation, rather than changing continuously in proportion to changes in the stimulus.

NOR gate: a logic circuit whose output is FALSE (zero) if any input is TRUE (one). *See also* Logic gate.

NOT gate: an inverter; a single-input logic circuit whose output is always the opposite of the input. That is, a TRUE (one) yields a FALSE (zero) and vice versa. *See also* Logic gate.

Optical computer: a computer in which light, rather than electricity, is the information-bearing medium.

Optical neural network: a neural network constructed of optical components.

Optimization problem: a mathematical problem in which the best of many possible solutions is sought; the classic example is that of a salesman seeking the shortest route to every city on an itinerary.

Optoelectronic: combining optical and electronic devices.

OR gate: a logic circuit whose output is TRUE (one) if any input is TRUE. *See also* Logic gate.

Output: the data sent from one device to another.

Parallel processing: in computing, the processing of data or instructions simultaneously, rather than sequentially.

Patch panel: a plugboard, resembling an old-fashioned telephone switchboard, in which interconnections are changed by moving the position of jumper wires; used to change the programming of early computers.

Perceptron: an early neural network, devised by psychologist Frank Rosenblatt in 1958.

Photon: the smallest increment of electromagnetic energy; most commonly applied to light.

Pico: the prefix denoting the one-trillionth part.

Polarization: the direction of vibration of light waves.

Quantum-well device: a semiconductor switch whose operation depends on the tendency of electrons to remain trapped in one layer of the device until they are freed by a pulse of energy. *See also* SEED.

Random-access memory (RAM): a form of computer memory, the contents of which can be altered by the user; it provides direct, rather than serial, access to all stored information.

Real-time computing: computer processing rapid enough to solve problems or control instruments as events occur.

Resistor: an electronic circuit component that restricts the flow of current.

Scaler: an analog-computer circuit that multiplies or divides values by a fixed number called a constant. *See also* Scaling.

Scaling: the practice of using one value to represent a larger or smaller one. *See also* Scaler.

SEED (Self Electro-optical Effect Device): a type of optical transistor. *See also* Quantum-well device.

Serial processing: the method of executing a program on a conventional, von Neumann computer, in which instructions are processed one at a time. *See also* Parallel processing.

Spatial light modulator (SLM): a device whose optical properties change in response to an outside stimulus, such as an electric current; the liquid crystal display of a calculator is one example.

Symbolic substitution logic: a method for processing data optically that substitutes an output pattern for an input pattern.

Threshold gate: in optical computing, a device that transmits light only when the beam exceeds a certain brightness.

Transistor: a semiconductor device that serves as either switch or amplifier; a basic building block of electronic circuits.

Transphasor: a type of optical transistor devised by Scottish physicist Desmond Smith in 1981.

Von Neumann architecture: the conventional computer design, in which operations are performed sequentially. *See also* Serial processing.

Von Neumann bottleneck: an operational slowdown in conventional computer designs, caused by the funneling of information into a single channel between the CPU and memory.

Waveguide: a conduit for radio and light waves. Optical fibers serve as waveguides of light; metal tubes are used to guide radio waves.

Bibliography

Books

Anderson, James A., and Edward Rosenfeld, editors, *Neurocomputing: Foundations of Research*. Cambridge, Massachusetts: The MIT Press, 1988.

Asimov, Isaac, *The Measure of the Universe*. New York: Harper & Row, Publishers, 1983.

Augarten, Stan, *Bit by Bit*. New York: Ticknor & Fields, 1984.

Berkeley, Edmund Callis, *Giant Brains or Machines That Think*. New York: Science Editions, 1961.

Boeke, Kees, *Cosmic View: The Universe in 40 Jumps*. New York: The John Day Company, 1957.

Bush, Vannevar, *Pieces of the Action*. New York: William Morrow and Company, 1970.

Ceruzzi, Paul E., *Reckoners: The Prehistory of the Digital Computer, from Relays to the Stored-Program Concept, 1935-1945*. Westport, Connecticut: Greenwood Press, 1983.

Dickerson, Richard E., and Irving Geis, *The Structure and Action of Proteins*. New York: Harper & Row, Publishers, 1969.

Drexler, K. Eric, *Engines of Creation*. New York: Doubleday, Anchor Press, 1986.

Durant, Will, *The Age of Faith*. New York: Simon and Schuster, 1950.

Feinberg, Gerald, and Robert Shapiro, *Life beyond Earth*. New York: William Morrow and Company, 1980.

Feitelson, Dror G., *Optical Computing: A Survey for Computer Scientists*. Cambridge, Massachusetts: The MIT Press, 1988.

Fifer, S., *Analogue Computation: Theory, Techniques and Applications*. 4 volumes. New York: McGraw-Hill Book Company, 1961.

Giloi, W. K., *Principles of Continuous System Simulation: Analog, Digital and Hybrid Simulation in a Computer Science Perspective*. Stuttgart, Germany: B. G. Teubner, 1975.

Goldstine, Herman H., *The Computer from Pascal to von Neumann*. Princeton, New Jersey: Princeton University Press, 1972.

Hartree, Douglas R., *Calculating Instruments and Machines*. Urbana, Illinois: The University of Illinois Press, 1949.

Hausner, A., *Analog and Hybrid Computer Programming*. Englewood Cliffs, New Jersey: Prentice-Hall, 1971.

Hyndman, D. E., *Analog and Hybrid Computing*. Oxford: Pergamon Press, 1970.

Jackson, A. S., *Analog Computation*. New York: McGraw-Hill Book Company, 1960.

Johnson, R. Colin, and Chappell Brown, *Cognizers: Neural Networks and Machines That Think*. New York: John Wiley & Sons, 1988.

Karplus, Walter J., and Walter W. Soroka, *Analog Methods: Computation and Simulation*. 2d edition. New York: McGraw-Hill Book Company, 1959.

Klimasauskas, Casimir, *NeuralWorks Professional II Reference Manual*. Sewickley, Pennsylvania: Neural Ware, Inc.

Korn, Granino A., and T. M. Korn, *Electronic Analog and Hybrid Computers*. New York: McGraw-Hill Book Company, 1964.

MacGregor, Ronald J., *Neural and Brain Modeling*. San Diego, California: Academic Press, 1987.

McLeod, John, editor, *Pioneers & Peers*. San Diego, California: Simulation Councils, Inc., 1988.

Millman, S., editor, *A History of Engineering & Science in the Bell System*. AT&T Bell Laboratories, 1984.

Minsky, Marvin, and Seymour Papert, *Perceptrons: An Introduction to Computational Geometry*. Expanded edition. Cambridge, Massachusetts: The MIT Press, 1988.

Morrison, Phillip, and Phylis Morrison, *Powers of Ten*. New York: Scientific American Books, 1982.

Pagels, Heinz R., *The Dreams of Reason: The Computer and the Rise of the Sciences of Complexity*. New York: Simon and Schuster, 1988.

Paynter, Henry M., editor, *A Palimpsest on the Electronic Analog Art*. Boston: George A. Philbrick Researches, Inc., 1955.

Photonics: Maintaining Competitiveness in the Information Era. Washington, D.C.: National Academy Press, 1988.

Rumelhart, David E., and James L. McClelland, *Parallel Distributed Processing*. Volume 1. Cambridge, Massachusetts: The MIT Press, 1986.

Shurkin, Joel, *Engines of the Mind*. New York: W. W. Norton & Company, 1984.

Space, by the Editors of Time-Life Books (Understanding Computers series). Alexandria, Virginia: Time-Life Books, 1987.

Stice, James E., and Bernet S. Swanson, *Electronic Analog Computer Primer*. New York: Blaisdell Publishing Company, 1965.

Tomovic, R., and W. J. Karplus, *High-Speed Analog Computers*. New York: John Wiley & Sons, 1962.

Truitt, Thomas D., and A. E. Rogers, *Basics of Analog Computers*. New York: John F. Rider Publisher, 1960.

Waldrop, M. Mitchell, *Man-Made Minds: The Promise of Artificial Intelligence*. New York: Walker and Company, 1987.

Warfield, John N., *Introduction to Electronic Analog Computers*. Englewood Cliffs, New Jersey: Prentice-Hall, 1959.

Weyrick, Robert C., *Fundamentals of Analog Computers*. Englewood Cliffs, New Jersey: Prentice-Hall, 1969.

Williams, Michael R., *A History of Computing Technology*. Englewood Cliffs, New Jersey: Prentice-Hall, 1985.

Periodicals

Allan, Roger, "The Inside News on Data Converters." *Electronics*, July 17, 1980.

Allman, William F., "The Computer with Many Heads." *U.S. News & World Report*, May 2, 1988.

Angier, Natalie, "The Organic Computer." *Discover*, May 1982.

Becker, Bill, "X-15 Flies 2,650 M.P.H., Cracking Record." *The New York Times*, March 8, 1961.

Bell, Trudy E., "Optical Computing: A Field in Flux." *IEEE Spectrum*, August 1986.

Bernstein, Jeremy, "Profiles: Marvin Minsky." *The New Yorker*, December 14, 1981.

Bradford, C. E., and W. M. Gaines, "Analog Computers—Successor to Cut and Try." *General Electric Review*, November 1953.

Brenner, Karl-Heinz, Alan Huang, and Norbert Streibl, "Digital Optical Computing with Symbolic Substitution." *Applied Optics,* September 15, 1986.

Carr, Joseph J., "Interfacing with an Analog World." Parts 1 and 2. *BYTE,* May 1977 and June 1977.

Caudill, Maureen, "Neural Networks Primer." Parts 1 and 2. *AI Expert,* December 1987 and February 1988.

Chithelen, Ignatius, "Teaching Computers." *Forbes,* February 8, 1988.

Ciarcia, Steve, "Build an Analog-to-Digital Converter." *BYTE,* January 1986.

Conrad, Michael, "The Lure of Molecular Computing." *IEEE Spectrum,* October 1986.

Cowan, Jack D., and David H. Sharp, "Neural Nets and Artificial Intelligence." *Daedalus,* winter 1988.

Crick, Francis, "The Recent Excitement about Neural Networks." *Nature,* January 12, 1989.

Dewdney, A. K.:
"Computer Recreations: Nanotechnology: Wherein Molecular Computers Control Tiny Circulatory Submarines." *Scientific American,* January 1988.
"Computer Recreations: On the Spaghetti Computer and Other Analog Gadgets for Problem Solving." *Scientific American,* June 1984.

Douglas, John H., "New Computer Architectures Tackle Bottleneck." *High Technology,* June 1983.

Drexler, Eric, "Mightier Machines from Tiny Atoms May Someday Grow." *Smithsonian,* November 1982.

Dreyfus, Stuart E.:
"Multi-Layer Neural Nets Recognize Regularities." *Applied Artificial Intelligence Reporter,* October 1987.
"Neural Nets: An Alternative Approach to AI." *Applied Artificial Intelligence Reporter*, September 1987.

"Electrical Gun Director Demonstrated." *Bell Laboratories Record,* November 1948.

Elmer-DeWitt, Philip, "Letting 1,000 Flowers Bloom." *Time,* June 9, 1986.

"Fast and Smart." *Time,* March 28, 1988.

Finkbeiner, Ann, "The Brain as Template." *Mosaic,* summer 1988.

Fitzgerald, Karen, "Whatever Happened to Analog Computers?" *IEEE Spectrum,* March 1987.

Froelich, Warren, "Dawn Glimmers for Day of the Man-Made Brain." *San Diego Union,* July 10, 1986.

Gilder, George, "You Ain't Seen Nothing Yet." *Forbes,* April 4, 1988.

Gorman, Christine, "Putting Brainpower in a Box." *Time,* August 8, 1988.

Graf, Hans P., Lawrence D. Jackel, and Wayne E. Hubbard, "VLSI Implementation of a Neural Network Model." *Computer,* March 1988.

Gutcho, Lynette, "DECtalk: A Year Later." *Speech Technology,* August/September 1985.

Hapgood, Fred, "Tiny Tech." *Omni,* December 1986.

Hartley, Karen, "Seeing the Need for 'ART.' " *Science News,* July 4, 1987.

Hecht, Jeff, "Optical Computers." *High Technology,* February 1987.

Hecht-Nielsen, Robert, "Neurocomputing: Picking the Human Brain." *IEEE Spectrum,* March 1988.

Heppenheimer, T. A.:
"Micro Micro Micro Chips." *Popular Science,* December 1986.
"Nerves of Silicon." *Discover,* February 1988.

Hillis, W. Daniel, "The Connection Machine." *Scientific American,* June 1987.

Hoffman, Paul, "The Next Leap in Computers." *The New York Times Magazine,* December 7, 1986.

Imse, Anne, "Microchips That Live?" *The Orange County Register,* May 22, 1988.

Johnson, George, "Artificial Brain Again Seen as a Guide to the Mind," *The New York Times,* August 16, 1988.

Johnson, R. Colin, and Tom J. Schwartz, "DARPA Backs Neural Nets." *Electronic Engineering Times,* August 8, 1988.

Jorgensen, Chuck, and Chris Matheus, "Catching Knowledge in Neural Nets." *AI Expert,* December 1986.

Kinoshita, June, and Nicholas G. Palevsky, "Computing with Neural Networks." *High Technology,* May 1987.

Klatt, Dennis, "Review of Text-to-Speech Conversion for English." *Journal of the Acoustical Society of America,* September 1987.

Kohonen, Teuvo, "The 'Neural' Phonetic Typewriter." *Computer,* March 1988.

Krauthammer, Charles, "The Joy of Analog." *Time,* May 26, 1986.

Larson, Erik, "Neural Chips." *OMNI,* September 1986.

Lemley, Brad, "Megachip." *The Washington Post Magazine,* January 6, 1985.

McCulloch, Warren, and Walter Pitts, "A Logical Calculus of the Ideas Immanent in Nervous Activity." *The Bulletin of Mathematical Biophysics,* December 1943.

Mayr, Otto, "The Origins of Feedback Control." *Scientific American,* October 1970.

"Miniaturisation Goes Mad." *The Economist,* May 24, 1986.

"Neural Networks May Someday Detect Forgers." *Computer,* March 1988.

Ostroff, Jim, "Biochips." *Venture,* February 1983.

Paynter, H. M., "In Memoriam: George A. Philbrick (1913-1974): A Brief Personal Tribute." *Journal of Dynamic Systems, Measurement, and Control,* June 1975.

Petre, Peter, "Speak, Master: Typewriters That Take Dictation." *Fortune,* January 7, 1985.

Pollack, Andrew:
"More Human than Ever, Computer Is Learning to Learn." *The New York Times,* September 15, 1987.
"New Chips Offer the Promise of Much Speedier Computers." *The New York Times,* January 4, 1989.
"U.S. Seeks Brain-Like Computers." *The New York Times,* August 18, 1988.

Port, Otis, "Computers That Come Awfully Close to Thinking."

Business Week, June 2, 1986.

Porter, Stephen, "Thinking Machines Redefine Computing." *Computer Graphics World,* August 1987.

Regis, Ed, "Interview: Eric Drexler." *Omni,* January 1989.

Richards, Michael, "Nanotechnology: Building a New World, Atom by Atom." *The Washington Post,* December 21, 1986.

"Rival." *The New Yorker,* December 6, 1958.

Robinson, Arthur L.:
"Multiple Quantum Wells for Optical Logic." *Science,* August 24, 1984.
"Nanocomputers from Organic Molecules?" *Science,* May 27, 1983.

Roger, Allan, "The Inside News on Data Converters." *Electronics,* July 17, 1980.

Rogers, Michael, "Mimicking the Human Mind." *Newsweek,* July 20, 1987.

Ross, Nancy L., "Mouth-to-Ear Interpretation." *The Washington Post,* February 24, 1989.

Sanger, David E., "A Computer Full of Surprises." *The New York Times,* May 8, 1987.

Schwartz, Tom J., "Bernard Widrow: Neural Network Pioneer." *Applied Artificial Intelligence Reporter,* October 1987.

Sejnowski, Terrence J., Christof Koch, and Patricia S. Churchland, "Computational Neuroscience." *Science,* September 9, 1988.

Sheingold, Daniel H., "George A. Philbrick: Gentleman, Innovator." *Electronic Design 3,* February 1, 1975.

Stipp, David, "Computer Researchers Find 'Neural Networks' Help Mimic the Brain." *The Wall Street Journal,* September 29, 1988.

Suplee, Curt, "Efforts to Duplicate Human 'Wetware': Is This Machine Thinking?" *The Washington Post,* March 3, 1987.

Tank, David W., and John J. Hopfield, "Collective Computation in Neuronlike Circuits." *Scientific American,* December 1987.

Tucker, Jonathan B., "Biochips: Can Molecules Compute?" *High Technology,* February 1984.

Tucker, Lewis W., and George G. Robertson, "Architecture and Applications of the Connection Machine." *Computer,* August 1988.

Van Brunt, Jennifer, "Biochips: The Ultimate Computer." *Bio/Technology,* March 1985.

Waltz, David L., "Applications of the Connection Machine." *Computer,* January 1987.

West, Lawrence C., "Picosecond Integrated Optical Logic." *Computer,* December 1987.

Williamson, Mickey, "Neural Networks: Glamour and Glitches." *Computerworld,* February 15, 1988.

Zeidenberg, Matthew, "Modeling the Brain." *BYTE,* December 1987.

Other Sources

Birge, Robert R., A. F. Lawrence, and L. A. Findsen, "Current Research and Future Potential of the Application of Molecular Electronics to Computer Architecture." Center for Molecular Electronics, Carnegie-Mellon University, no date.

"Connection Machine® Model CM-2 Technical Summary." Thinking Machines Technical Report HA87-4, April 1987.

DARPA Neural Network Study, October 1987-February 1988, Executive Summary, July 8, 1988.

Drexler, K. Eric, "Exploring Future Technologies." *The Reality Club,* Volume 1, 1988.

Eames, the Office of Charles and Ray, *A Computer Perspective.* Cambridge, Massachusetts: Harvard University Press, 1973.

Landauer, J. Paul, "Engineering Requirements for Real-Time Aerospace Simulation." Paper presented at the 1987 AIAA Aerospace Engineering Conference.

Rosenfeld, Edward, "Neurocomputing—A New Industry." *Proceedings of the IEEE First Annual International Conference on Neural Networks,* June 1987.

Sejnowski, Terrence J., and Charles R. Rosenberg:
"NETtalk: A Parallel Network That Learns to Read Aloud." *The Johns Hopkins University Electrical Engineering and Computer Science Technical Report, JHU/EECS-86-01, 1986.*
"Parallel Networks That Learn to Pronounce English Text." *Complex Systems 1 (1987).*

Thomas, Linnis G., Jr., "Simulation of Space Shuttle Main Engine." Paper presented at conference of the Society for Computer Simulation International, Seattle, Washington, July 1988.

Will, Craig A., "Neural Network Architectures and Their Implications for Next Generation Information Systems." *Next Generation Information Systems: Technology for the Future, Proceedings of the ACM/NBS 26th Annual Technical Symposium,* June 1987.

Acknowledgments

The editors of Time-Life Books wish to thank the following individuals and institutions for their assistance in the preparation of this volume: **In France**: Vernon—Philippe Ansart, Philippe Buffet, and Jean-Claude Vinot, Société Européenne de Propulsion. **In the United States**: Alabama—Huntsville: Linnis Thomas, Marshall Space Flight Center; Redstone Arsenal: Kelly Grider, U.S. Army Missile Command; Arizona—Tucson: Hyatt Gibbs, University of Arizona; Granino A. Korn; Arkansas—Fayetteville: Maurice E. McCoy; California—Los Angeles: George Bekey, University of Southern California; Malibu: Yuri Owechko and Bernard Soffer, Hughes Research Laboratories; Mountain View: Judith Dayhoff; Jack Sherman; Pasadena: Carver Mead, California Institute of Technology; Redondo Beach: Timothy L. Dolan and Mike Myers, TRW Electronics Systems Group; San Diego: Robert Hecht-Nielsen; Santa Monica: Boris Kogan; Stanford: Joseph W. Goodman and Bernard Widrow, Stanford University; Van Nuys: William Ross, Litton Data Systems; District of Columbia—Paul Ceruzzi, Smithsonian Institution; Arthur Fisher, Naval Research Laboratory; C. Lee Giles, Air Force Office of Scientific Research; Harold Szu, Naval Research Laboratory; Paul Werbos, National Science Foundation; Illinois—Barrington: Ray H. Spiess, Comdyna, Inc.; Evanston: Mark Ratner, Northwestern University; Maryland—Annapolis: Ronald E. Siatkowski, U.S. Naval Academy; College Park: Kenneth R. Stephens, BehavHeuristics, Inc.; Jim Reggia, University of Maryland; Kensington: Jane Gruenebaum; Massachusetts—Cambridge: Sally Beddow, MIT Museum; Dennis Klatt; Susan Worst, MIT Press; Lexington: Alan Grometstein, M.I.T. Lincoln Labs; Norwood: Daniel H. Sheingold, Analog Devices, Inc.; Waltham: Jeffrey Fried, GTE Labs; Michigan—Ann Arbor: Gene Graber, Applied Dynamics International; Robert Howe and Emmett Leith, University of Michigan; Missouri—St. Louis: Mary Ambos and Nicole Van Opdenbosch, Tripos Associates; Nevada—Zephyr Cove: Peter S. Guilfoyle, Opticomp Corporation; New Jersey—Basking Ridge: Kevin Compton, AT&T; Hillsdale: Julia Hough, Lawrence Erlbaum Publishers; Red Bank: Peter Smith, Bellcore; Short Hills: Ed Eckert, Alan Huang, David Miller, Mike Miller, and Joy Perillo, AT&T Bell Labs; New York—New York: Karen Fitzgerald, Institute of Electrical and Electronic Engineers; Edward Rosenfeld, Intelligence Newsletter; Syracuse: Robert R. Birge, Syracuse University; Yorktown Heights: Ari Aviram and Alan Fowler, IBM Watson Research Center; Pennsylvania—Doylestown: Per Holst; Virginia—Alexandria: Craig Will, Institute for Defense Analyses; Arlington: Dwight Duston, SDI Innovative Science Technology Directorate; McLean: Robert Clerman, MITRE Corporation.

Picture Credits

The sources for the illustrations that appear in this book are listed below. Credits from left to right are separated by semicolons; from top to bottom they are separated by dashes.

Cover: Art by Lili Robins. 6-9: Art by Lili Robins. 12, 13: The MIT Museum. 14: Courtesy AT&T Archives. 17-23: Art by Sam Ward. 25, 29: Art by Lili Robins. 31-39: Art by Matt McMullen. 40-43: Art by Matt McMullen, based on illustrations by Gabor Kiss on page 112 of "Collective Computation in Neuronlike Circuits," by David W. Tank and John J. Hopfield, *Scientific American*, December 1987. 44: Art by Lili Robins. 46: Biophoto Associates/Science Source, Photo Researchers; CNRI/Science Photo Library, Photo Researchers. 47, 49: Art by Lili Robins. 50: Courtesy the Rosenblatt family and the estate of Frank Rosenblatt. 51: Calvin Campbell, MIT News Office. 52, 53: Art by Lili Robins. 54: Max Aguilera-Hellweg/Onyx. 56, 57: Art by Al Kettler. 58, 59: Art by John Drummond. 61: Courtesy HNC, Inc. 63, 64: Art by Lili Robins. 67: Courtesy TRW MEAD Neural Network Center, San Diego. 69-83: Art by Stephen R. Wagner. 84-87: Art by Lili Robins. 88: Chuck O'Rear. 90, 91: Art by Lili Robins. 93: Courtesy Unisys Corporation. 94-97: Art by Lili Robins. 98-103: Art by Al Kettler. 104, 105: Art by Lili Robins. 106: New York Times Pictures. 107: Susan Spann. 109: Background art by Matt McMullen. 111-118: Art by Bryan Leister, photographed by Larry Sherer.

125

Index

Numerals in italics indicate an illustration of the subject mentioned.

Time-Life Books Inc.
is a wholly owned subsidiary of
TIME INCORPORATED

FOUNDER: Henry R. Luce 1898-1967

Editor-in-Chief: Jason McManus
Chairman and Chief Executive Officer:
J. Richard Munro
President and Chief Operating Officer:
N. J. Nicholas, Jr.
Editorial Director: Richard B. Stolley
Executive Vice President, Books: Kelso F. Sutton
Vice President, Books: Paul V. McLaughlin

TIME-LIFE BOOKS INC.

EDITOR: George Constable
Executive Editor: Ellen Phillips
Director of Design: Louis Klein
Director of Editorial Resources: Phyllis K. Wise
Editorial Board: Russell B. Adams, Jr.,
Dale M. Brown, Roberta Conlan, Thomas H.
Flaherty, Lee Hassig, Donia Ann Steele,
Rosalind Stubenberg
Director of Photography and Research:
John Conrad Weiser
Assistant Director of Editorial Resources:
Elise Ritter Gibson

PRESIDENT: Christopher T. Linen
Chief Operating Officer: John M. Fahey, Jr.
Senior Vice Presidents: Robert M. DeSena,
James L. Mercer, Paul R. Stewart
Vice Presidents: Stephen L. Bair, Ralph J. Cuomo,
Neal Goff, Stephen L. Goldstein, Juanita T. James,
Carol Kaplan, Susan J. Maruyama, Robert H. Smith,
Joseph J. Ward
Director of Production Services: Robert J. Passantino
Supervisor of Quality Control: James King

Editorial Operations
Copy Chief: Diane Ullius
Production: Celia Beattie
Library: Louise D. Forstall

Correspondents: Elisabeth Kraemer-Singh (Bonn);
Christine Hinze (London); Christina Lieberman (New
York); Maria Vincenza Aloisi (Paris); Ann Natanson
(Rome); Dick Berry (Tokyo). Valuable assistance was
also provided by: Elizabeth Brown (New York); Lesley
Coleman (London).

UNDERSTANDING COMPUTERS

SERIES DIRECTOR: Lee Hassig
Series Administrators: Loretta Britten, Gwen Mullen

Editorial Staff for *Alternative Computers*
Designer: Lorraine D. Rivard
Associate Editors: Kristin Baker Hanneman (pictures),
Allan Fallow (text)
Researchers: Steven Feldman, Flora J. Garcia, Char-
lotte Fullerton
Writer: Robert M. S. Somerville
Assistant Designer: Tessa Tilden-Smith
Copy Coordinator: Elizabeth Graham
Picture Coordinator: Robert H. Wooldridge, Jr.
Editorial Assistant: Susan L. Finken

Special Contributors: Bill Allman, Jeff Hecht, Tom
Heppenheimer, Jim Merritt, John Rubin, Daniel
Stashower (text); Julianne Lammersen Baum, Sydney
Johnson (research); Mel Ingber (index)

THE CONSULTANTS

JAMES A. ANDERSON, a professor of psychology and
cognitive and linguistic sciences at Brown University, is
exploring the theory and applications of neural-network
computers. He is the coeditor of *Neurocomputing: Foundations of Research.*

ROBERT R. BIRGE teaches chemistry at Syracuse University, where he directs the Center for Molecular Electronics. He is investigating the use of proteins in optical-
computer memories and high-speed optical switches.

H. JOHN CAULFIELD directs the Center for Applied Optics at the University of Alabama in Huntsville.

K. ERIC DREXLER, a research engineer, is president of the
nonprofit educational organization the Foresight Institute. He is the author of *Engines of Creation.*

BRIAN HAYES has written about computers and computing for such periodicals as *Scientific American, BYTE,*
and *Computer Language.*

JOHN J. HOPFIELD, a physicist, splits his time between
the California Institute of Technology and AT&T Bell
Laboratories. His research covers a number of fields,
including neurobiology, neural networks, and biological
molecules.

WALTER J. KARPLUS, a professor of computer science at
the University of California in Los Angeles, has written
extensively about analog computers.

ROBERT M. KUCZEWSKI is a researcher at the TRW
Military Electronics and Avionics Division. He is studying
the application of neural networks in pattern recognition
and related fields.

J. PAUL LANDAUER is the chief systems architect at
Electronic Associates, Inc., a simulation-computer company based in West Long Branch, New Jersey.

JAMES H. McALEAR has been advocating a national ini-
tiative on molecular electronics since 1975.

JOHN McLEOD, an engineer, founded the Society for
Computer Simulation International in San Diego, California. He is also editor emeritus of the journal *Simulation.*

HENRY M. PAYNTER, an emeritus professor of mechanical engineering at M.I.T., served as director of the American Center for Analog Computing in Boston, Massachusetts, from 1950 to 1960.

EDWARD ROSENFELD is editor and publisher of *Intelligence,* a monthly publication devoted to developments
in the research and commercialization of neural networks. He is also the coeditor, with James Anderson, of
Neurocomputing: Foundations of Research.

TERRENCE J. SEJNOWSKI, one of the developers of the
NETtalk neural network, is a professor at the University
of California at San Diego. He is also a director of the
Laboratory of Computational Neurobiology at the Salk
Institute in La Jolla, California.

GUY L. STEELE, a senior scientist at Thinking Machines
Corporation in Cambridge, Massachusetts, directs software design for the Connection Machine.

JOHN M. WEHRUNG, president of Gentronix Laboratories in Rockville, Maryland, is pursuing the development of molecular-electronic materials and biosensors.

MICHAEL R. WILLIAMS, a professor of computer science
at the University of Calgary in Canada, is the author of *A
History of Computing Technology.*

Library of Congress Cataloging in Publication Data

Alternative Computers / by the editors of Time-Life Books
   p.   cm.—(Understanding computers)
  Bibliography: p.
  Includes index.
  ISBN 0-8094-5745-8
  1. Computers.   I. Time-Life Books.   II. Series.
QA76.A565 1989   004—dc19   88-29512
                                       CIP

ISBN 0-8094-5746-6 (lib. bdg.)

For information on and a full description of any of the Time-
Life Books series listed, please write:
Reader Information
Time-Life Customer Service
P.O. Box C-32068
Richmond, Virginia 23261-2068